The Illustrated American Tourist Guide to English English

Second Edition

by
J. Eric Smithburn

authorHOUSE™

1663 Liberty Drive, Suite 200
Bloomington, Indiana 47403
(800) 839-8640
www.AuthorHouse.com

First published by AuthorHouse 04/21/05

ISBN: 1-4208-3846-6 (sc)

Library of Congress Control Number: 2005902481

Printed in the United States of America
Bloomington, Indiana

This book is printed on acid-free paper.

To Robin and Jenny Spon-Smith

Foreword

Suddenly you are lost. All around you there are folk speaking English. But it is difficult to understand half of what they are saying. Can they really be English people? The answer is probably yes, but you need help.

My old friend and scholar, J. Eric Smithburn, has written a remarkable guide for your benefit. It has three special qualities. It is useful, instructive and entertaining. It is your guide through the maze of language. No longer need you be lost. And even if you are, at least you can have an enjoyable read on the way.

This guide has been written mainly for American tourists, but it will be of interest and use to English-speaking people everywhere, including visitors to the United States.

Now the Guide is yours. Enjoy! Get weaving!

His Honour Neil Butter, CBE, QC
London
February 2005

Preface

After living in England off and on for over twenty years, I've come to realize that George Bernard Shaw was right when he said that the English and Americans are two people separated by a common language. The American visitor to England will every day hear words, phrases and expressions which are foreign to Americans, and yet should be understood to feel the complete texture of one's travel experience in Britain.

The material in the book comes from all segments of English society and will equip the tourist to understand words and expressions common in the pub, on television, in the broadsheets (there's one), at athletic contests, or in more formal settings. The words and expressions are common throughout England, and no attempt has been made to include words from specific cities or regions of the country, nor has the outdated Cockney rhyming slang been included (except for a few expressions that are common in modern conversation).

The book features the English word or expression opposite the American meaning. If there is no American counterpart for the English word or expression, the English definition is provided.

My interest in writing this guide began in the early 1980s with conversations over tea at Bryanston Square with Vivienne Simmonds. The manuscript has been enriched over the years by contributions from Pat Beaver, Bruce Blair, Roy and Jill Bridges, Meg Ceriani, Leo Cookson, John Finnis, Chris and Christine Gane, Neil Butter and Claire Miskin, Robin Morse, Jack Pratt, John Pearson, Gillian Walker and Linda Wilbram. Special thanks go to Peter and Mary Carey, Jenny and Robin Spon-Smith and Geoffrey Bennett for their help. Thanks also to Sharon Loftus for her excellent typing assistance.

J. Eric Smithburn

THE ILLUSTRATED AMERICAN TOURIST GUIDE TO ENGLISH ENGLISH

Second Edition

J. Eric Smithburn

ENGLISH   **AMERICAN**

A

access (legal) (see contact)	visitation with minor children
acclimatised	acclimated
ace	top notch
across the river (*gone ... ...*) (*see* passed over)	died
act for	represent (usually in a legal capacity)
acting common	not doing something properly, lacking style
adjournment	to continue proceedings until another time
advert	advertisement

English	American
aerial (*television*)	antenna
afternoon tea	served at around 4:00 p.m., includes finger sandwiches, scones, cookies and dessert such as a fruit tart or rich cake
afters	dessert
aggro	aggravation
air hostess	flight attendant, stewardess
airing cupboard	closet including water heater
airy-fairy	flakey, spacey
A-levels	graded academic tests, the results of which are used to apply for admission to university
all beer and skittles	excellent
all champagne and opera	excellent
all in	tired
all in (*menu or tariff*)	meals included
allotment	plot of ground leased for growing flowers or vegetables

English	American
Alsatian	German Shepherd
America	the United States or U.S.
amongst	among
ancillary staff	not involved in company's main business, non-policy-making staff
ankle socks	bobby socks
anorak	parka
anorak (*he's an ...*)	person obsessed with something regarded as boring (e.g. computer geek)
answerphone (*message on my ...*)	voicemail, message machine
anti-clockwise	counter-clockwise
AOB	any other business
aperitif	alcoholic beverage before a meal
application	request for action
apprentice waiter	bus boy
arches (*motor car*) (*see* wing)	fenders (car)

English	American
Argie	Argentine, Argentinian
argy-bargy	commotion, loud argument
aristobabble	upper class conversation
aristos	aristocrats
arse	ass
arse-licker (*see* bum-licker, toady)	ass-kisser, brown-nose

arse-licker

arsey (*person*)	difficult
arsey-versy	back to front

English	American
artic (*abbr.* articulated lorry)	semi-truck, eighteen wheeler
articulated lorry (*see artic*)	semi-truck with separate cabin adjoined to rear, eighteen wheeler
aspic	savory jelly used to coat or garnish food
assessment (*academic*)	grading
at a stroke	immediately and easily (as with the stroke of a pen)
at the weekend	over the weekend
athletics	non-aquatic sporting events
attainment (*academic ...*)	achievement
aubergine	eggplant
autumn	fall
away (*he is ...*)	gone
a word (*May I have ... ...?*)	speak with
A word?	May I speak with you?
ay(e)	yes

English	American
B	
backbencher	Member of Parliament who does not hold office in the government or opposition
back-comb (*hair*)	tease
backhander	bribe
backside (*see* bum)	bottom, buttocks, butt, rear end
backwoodsman	a non-participating member of the House of Lords (usually an hereditary peer) who attends House proceedings to vote on an important matter
bad form (*that's ... ...*)	inappropriate behavior
bad hat (*he's a ... ...*)	disreputable person (possibly criminal)
BAFTA Awards	equivalent to American "Oscars"
bags of time	plenty (loads, lots) of time
bain marie	double boiler
balloon's gone up	some trouble has begun
balls up (*n.*)	screw up, mess

The Illustrated American Tourist Guide to English English

English	American
banana skin (*turn into a ... ...*)	risky situation
banged up	in jail

banged up

| banged up (*see in the club, preg, preggy, preggers, up the duff*) | pregnant |

English	American
banger	old car
banger	sausage
bangers and mash	sausages and mashed potatoes
bangles	ornamental colored jewelry worn in hair or on wrist
bang-on (see spot-on)	exactly right, on the money
bang-opposite	directly opposite
bank holiday	official holiday
bank note	bill
bap	bun (hamburger) or large bread roll
baphead	idiotic person
bargaining counter	bargaining chip
barge pole (wouldn't touch it with a ... ...)	want nothing to do with it, wouldn't touch it with a ten-foot pole
barmy	crazy, nuts
barney	fight, quarrel
barrack (v.)	verbally assault

English	American
barrister	trial lawyer
bat (*ping pong*)	paddle
bath (*in the ...*)	bathtub
batsman	one who bats (cricket)
battels (*university*)	charges on account
batting for (*cricket metaphor*)	effort in behalf of someone or something
BBC	British Broadcasting Corporation
be on (*he'll ... ... to you*)	understand
be upstanding (*court*) (*see upstanding*)	please rise
beak	magistrate
beaker	mug
beans on toast	common English breakfast selection
beavering	working hard
bed of nails	booby trap
bed-sit	own bedroom, share facilities

English	American
beeb	nickname for the British Broadcasting Corporation (BBC)
beefeater	yeoman warder at the Tower of London
beer mat	coaster
begin again	start over
Belisha beacon	round blinking orange light at a pedestrian crosswalk
below stairs	dated reference to servants employed in upper class household
belt up	shut up
belter	very hot day
belting down	raining hard

belting down

English	American
bends	serious physical condition from changing depth too fast in deep sea diving
benefit (*on ...*)	welfare, public assistance
bent	gay, homosexual
bent (*is ...*)	dishonest, corrupt
berk (*You ...!*)	fool
besotted (*... with*)	smitten
bespoke	custom made
bespoke tailor	a tailor who makes clothes from cloth to finish, custom tailor
bettle (*... off*)	go away, slip away
big dipper	roller coaster
big ends (*motor car*)	main bearings (automobile)
bill (*restaurant*)	check, tab
bill (*the ...*) (*see* old bill)	the police
bill of fare	menu
bin	trash can, waste basket

English	American
bin bag	trash bag
bin it	throw in the trash, discard
bin liner	trash bag
binman (*see dustman*)	garbage or trash collector
bird	woman, girl
bird spike	bird feeder on a pole
Biro	ballpoint pen
biscuit (*sweet*)	cookie
biscuit (*unsweetened, savoury*)	cracker
bit (*the next ..., that ..., this...*)	point, thing, information
bits (*the other ...*)	things, parts
bits and bobs (*see bits and pieces*)	small amount
bits and pieces (*see bits and pieces*)	small amount
bitter	tepid beer composed of barley, hops and yeast
bitter and twisted	upset

English	American
Black Maria . (see police van)	former name for police vehicle used to transport persons (to the police station)
black spot	place on a road where accidents frequently occur
black treacle (see treacle)	molasses
blackleg	scab, strike breaker
blag	talk your way into something
blagger	person who works at a carnival
blast (Oh ...!)	damn
bleeding (see bloody)	damned
bless their (your) cotton socks	bless their (your) hearts
blighter (see rotter)	despicable person
Blimey! (see Crikey! Gorblimey!)	expression of surprise such as Son-of-a-gun! or Gee whiz!
blind (window)	shade
blinkers (... on the horse)	blinders

English	American
block of flats	apartment house or building
bloke	man, boy
blood is up	angry
blood sport	sport involving the killing of animals (*e.g.* fox hunting, hare coursing)
bloody (*see bleeding*)	very, damned
bloody-minded	being difficult, stubborn with slight hostility
bloomer	long loaf of bread
bloomer	mistake
blooming (*move your ...*)	damned
blot on your escutcheon (*see escutcheon*)	disgrace your honor or reputation
blot your copybook	caught doing something wrong
blotto	extremely drunk
blow the gaff (*see give the game away*)	divulge a secret
blow your own trumpet	blow (toot) your own horn

English	American
blowsy	flashy, overblown (a woman)
blue arsed fly (b.a.f.)	chasing, moving around, working hard
blue joke	off color, dirty joke
blue rinse brigade	elderly ladies who are conservative in manner and view
bob	one shilling (pre-decimalization), now five pence
bob or two (*worth a ... ...*)	a lot of money
bobby	police officer
bobish (*adj.*)	upbeat, cheerful
body swerve	dodge
boffin	scientist
bog	toilet, bathroom
bogey	booger, snot
boiled sweet	hard candy
bold as brass	brash

English	American
bollard	mechanically operated steel column or post which rises from below the pavement and serves as a road barrier
bollocking (*gave him a right ...*) (*see* rollicking)	tell off, read someone the riot act
bollock-naked	stark naked
bollocks (*load of ...*)	bunch of crap
bolshie	aggressive, boorish
bomb (*it cost a ...*)	large amount of money, expensive
bomb (*the performance was a ...*)	smash hit
bone idle	extremely lazy
bone-shaker	old car, rattle trap (originally an early design of bicycle)
bonk (*v.*)	have sexual intercourse
bonking (*n.*)	sexual intercourse
bonnet	hood of a car
book (*v.*)	make a reservation

English	American
booking (n.)	reservation
booking office	ticket office
bookshop	bookstore
boot (n.)	athletic shoe
boot (n.)	trunk of car
boot on the other foot	shoe on the other foot
boot sale (see car boot sale)	sale from car trunk (like yard or garage sale)
bootlace	shoestring
boozer (local ...)	bar, tavern
bop off	bump off, kill
borstal	penal institution for juveniles
bossyboots	bossy person, control freak
bottle (he's a full ... on that)	has a lot of information
bottle (he has a lot of ...)	courage
bottom (he's got ...)	gravitas, status, weight
bottom (... of the street)	end

English	American
bottom drawer (*bride's ... ...*)	hope chest
bottom of the cage	depressed
bounder	untrustworthy person, cad
bovril (*... on toast*)	beef spread on bread
Bow bells (*see Cockney*)	bells of Bow Cathedral in East London
bowled out (*cricket metaphor*)	defeated, completely deflated
bowler (*hat*)	derby
bowling green (*see bowls*)	lawn for playing bowls
bowls (*see bowling green*)	game with hard heavy ball (bowl) played outdoors on grass; a small ball (jack) is bowled to a random spot at the far end of the green; players roll bowls (which are biased so they don't roll in a straight line) to get as close as possible to the jack (which may involve knocking someone else's bowl away); the player whose bowl ends up nearest the jack wins (also called crown green bowls)

English	American
bowser (*airport*)	fuel truck
box (*see* goggle box)	television
Boxing Day	the day after Christmas
braces	suspenders for pants
bracket(s) (*see* round brackets, square brackets)	mark used in pairs (parentheses or brackets) for enclosing words or figures
brain around (*get my ... ...*)	understand
brainbox	intelligent person
brass (*n.*)	prostitute
brass neck	a lot of nerve
brass you off	annoy, irritate
brassed off (*see* browned off, cheesed off)	fed up
break down (*car*)	engine trouble, stalled
brick (*real ...*)	solid, reliable person
brickie	bricklayer
bride's bottom drawer	hope chest
bridge roll	sandwich bun

English	American
bridle way	a path reserved for horse riding
brief	task, assignment
briefs	undershorts
brill (*abbr.* brilliant)	outstanding, very good
brilliant (*see* brill)	outstanding, very good
bring forward	introduce
bring to book	bring to justice
Brit (*abbr.* Briton)	person from Great Britain
Briton (*see* Brit)	person from Great Britain
broad bean	lima bean
broad church	wide range of issues
broadsheets	non-tabloid newspapers
broken down (*he's ... ...*)	car trouble
broll (*abbr.* brolly)	umbrella
brolly (*see* broll)	umbrella
brothel-creepers	suede or soft-soled shoes
brought up	stopped abruptly

English	American
browned off (see brassed off, cheesed off)	thoroughly fed up
Brummie	person from Birmingham
bubble and squeak	mix of mashed potatoes and cabbage fried
bubbly (glass of ...)	champagne
buck out	avoid
bucket of sand	something of no value, worthless
bucketing (... rain)	pouring
budgerigar (see budgie)	parakeet
budgie (abbr. budgerigar)	parakeet
buffer	front and rear protective parts (steel plates) of a train
buffer (silly old ...)	narrow-minded elderly man
bugger	unpleasant or difficult person
bugger off (Oh, ...!)	shove off, don't bother me
building society	savings and loan

English	American
bullet (*n.*)	notice of termination, pink slip
bullet point	specially marked point
bullying	beating by bully at school
bum (*see backside*)	bottom, butt, buttocks, rear end
bum-licker (*see arse-licker, toady*)	ass-kisser, brown-nose
bumper	alcoholic drink
bumpf (*the ...*)	excessive unimportant written information
bums on seats	fill up arena or theatre
bun	drunken state
bun fight	mass of people scrambling to do the same thing
bun in the oven	pregnant

bun in the oven

English	American
bundle	packet of papers (not newspapers) bound together
bung	bribe
bung (*see* chuck)	throw or put
bunged	made pregnant, knocked up
bunged up (*nose is ... ...*)	blocked, stuffed up
bung-eyed	sleepy-eyed
bunk off (*see* did a bunk)	not show up for a commitment, a no-show
bunkum	nonsense
bunting	decorative flags
burgled	burglarized
busk (*v.*) (*see* busker)	entertaining as a busker
busker (*n.*) (*see* busk)	street entertainer
bust-up (*see* dust-up)	verbal confrontation, often followed by a temporary parting of the ways
butcher's (*a quick ...*)	look (originally, butcher's hook was Cockney rhyming slang for look)

English	American
butter muslin	cheesecloth
buttery	business (or room at a university) where food and drink are sold
buttie (*bacon ...*)	sandwich
by dint of	by means of, by virtue of
By Heck!	Wow!
by-election	election held during Parliament to fill a vacant seat

C

C of E	Church of England
cabbage cleaner	money launderer
cack-handed (*... ... move*)	clumsy, awkward
cadge	borrow
call (*train will ... at*)	stop
call box (*see* phone box, phone kiosk)	phone booth
call minder (*BT ... ...*)	company voice mail

English	American
call up	draft into military service
called (*his son is ... John*)	named
came around	came over
came up trumps	luck, good fortune
camp (*see* high camp)	outwardly gay
camp bed	cot
candy floss	cotton candy
cane (*v.*) (*the teacher will... him*)	paddle
canoodle	hugging and kissing another person, making out
can't be bothered	don't want to do something
cap fits (*if the ... ...*)	if the shoe fits wear it
caper	trick
car boot sale (*see* boot sale)	sale from car trunk (like yard or garage sale)
car hire	auto rental
car park	parking lot, parking garage

English	American
car sharing	car pooling
caravan	trailer

caravan

English	American
caravan site	trailer park
caravanette	recreational vehicle (r.v.)
cardy (*abbr.* cardigan)	cardigan
caretaker	janitor
carpeted (*see* matted)	disciplined
carriage (*train*)	car
carriageway (*see* dual carriageway)	highway, road
carry on	continue, go ahead
carry the can	take the blame
case	briefcase

English	American
caster sugar	superfine sugar
casualty	emergency room, ER
cat among the pigeons (*put the ... ...*)	cause turmoil
catapult	slingshot
catch a cold	criticized for a mistake
catch out (*cricket metaphor*) (*see* caught out)	point out a mistake (in a critical manner), found doing something wrong
catch you up	catch up with you
Catherine wheel	pinwheel
cat's-eye	reflective light on road to indicate traffic lanes
caught out (*cricket metaphor*) (*see* catch out)	point out a mistake (in a critical manner), found doing something wrong
CBE	Commander of the British Empire
celeriac	celery-like vegetable with edible root
central reservation	median strip
centre refuge	safe island in the middle of the road

English	American
certain age (of a ... ...)	older person
CH	central heating
chalk from cheese	completely different
chamber maid	cleaning lady at a hotel
chambers (member of ...)	set of barristers' offices
changing room	dressing room
chap (decent ...)	fellow, man, boy
charlie (see wally, wuss)	stupid in the non-derogatory sense
charwoman	cleaning lady
chase up (I'll ... him ...) (see get on to)	chase down, track down, contact a person
chat (v.)	talk to
chat back	strong exchange of words
chat box (abbr. chatterbox)	one who talks too much
chat show	talk show
chat show host	talk show host
chat up	flirt, talk with member of opposite sex

English	American
Chatham House Rules	off the record
chattering classes	disparaging reference to writers, politicians and intellectuals
cheek	nerve
cheek by jowl	close together
cheeky	brash, nervy
cheeky bugger	insolent person
cheerio (see cheers, toodle pip)	goodbye
Cheers (see cheerio, toodle pip)	goodbye
Cheers!	here's to you (toast)
cheesed off (see brassed off, browned off)	thoroughly fed up, annoyed, teed off
cheesey bits	hors d'oeuvres, snacks
cheesey feet	bad smelling feet
chemist	druggist, pharmacist
chemist shop	drugstore, pharmacy
chervil	carrot-like vegetable with edible leaves

English	American
Chesterfield	couch (leather) with padded back, seat and ends
chesty (... *cold*)	chest
chicken salad	piece of chicken with fresh vegetables
chicory	endive
chin-wag	chat, conversation
chip shop (*see* chippy)	fast food outlet that sells fish and chips
chipper	feeling well
chippy	carpenter
chippy (*see* chip shop)	fast food outlet that sells fish and chips
chips	French fried potatoes, fries
chirpy (*feel* ...)	feel well
chit	receipt, bill used as receipt
chivvy(ing)	actively encourage
choc	chocolate candy
choc-ice	ice cream bar coated in chocolate

English	American
chock	wooden block to hold a boat upright in dry dock or to keep an airplane from rolling
chock à block	completely full
chocks away	let's go
choked	upset or angry
choky	jail, prison
chop and change	change one's mind
chop chop!	hurry up
Christian name	first name
chuck (*see* bung)	throw or put
chuck away	throw away
chuff (*n.*)	butt, buttocks
chuffed (*... to bits*)	thrilled, delighted, pleased
chuffed to bollocks	very pleased
chum	friend, pal
chunder (*to ...*)	vomit
CHW	constant hot water

English	American
cigar ends	cigar butts
ciggie	cigarette
cinema	the movies, the show, movie theater
city centre (see town centre)	downtown
city farm	farm in urban area to expose children to farm animals and way of life
civil servant	government employee
civil service	permanently employed government bureaucracy who serve the elected ministers and other officials (excluding the judiciary and military)
claimant	plaintiff
clamp (v.)	police fasten disabling device to wheel of parked car
clanger (drop a ...)	make an embarrassing mistake
clapped out (esp. machinery)	worn out

English	American
claw back	take back something previously granted or paid
clean (... *teeth*)	brush
clean sheet of paper	start from scratch
clear (*v.*)	remove contents
clear of	ahead
clearway	stretch of freeway on which motorist may stop only in emergency
clever	smart, intelligent
clever-clogs (*you're a ... ...*)	smart person
clingfilm	plastic wrap
cloakroom	toilet and wash basin
clobber (*see* kit)	personal belongings
clock up	accumulate (years, points, etc.)
close to the wind	risky, politically incorrect
clot (*see* nana)	stupid person
cloth cap (*see* flat cap)	reference to working class person, particularly a trade union member

English	American
clothes peg	clothes pin
clotted cream	thick cream with a consistency similar to soft butter and served with jam on scones
cloud cuckoo land	out of touch with reality
clout	hit, strike a blow
clued up	informed
coach	bus
cob	jetty
cob	round loaf of bread
cob (*get a ... on*)	get angry
cobble up (*v.*)	to throw something together (e.g. a meal)
cobbler (*see slusher, monopoly man*)	counterfeiter
cobblers (*complete ...*)	nonsense
cock	rooster
cock a snook	thumb one's nose, show contempt
cock it up (*v.*)	screw it up

English	American
cock up (*n.*) (*a bloody ... ...*)	mess
cock-a-hoop	to be extremely pleased
cocked hat (*knocked into a ... ...*)	knocked down or out
Cockney (*see Bow bells*)	native of East London (born within the sound of the bells of Bow Cathedral)
codswallop (*a lot of ...*)	nonsense
collar felt (*have your ... ...*)	arrested and questioned by the police, pinched

have your collar felt

collar stud	collar button
collect (*v.*) (*... you at seven*)	pick up

English	American
collywobbles	intestinal noises or uncomfortable feeling
colonial	person from former British colony
come a cropper	to fall (physically or metaphorically)
come on to (*time*) (... ... ... *6:00 p.m.*)	shortly before
commentary box	press box
common room	meeting place, typically in a college or university
completion (*real estate*)	closing
comprehensive school	secondary school for children of all abilities
confectioner	candy store
conk	nose
conker	horse chestnut
conscript (*military*)	draftee
conscription (*see* national service)	military draft in wartime
conserve	preserves, jam
conspectus	overall view of the situation

English	American
consultant	medical specialist
contact (*legal*) (see access)	visitation with minor children
continental quilt (see duvet)	comforter (used on top of a sheet in lieu of a blanket)
cooker	stove
cooler	prison
copper bottomed (... ... *guarantee*)	foolproof
coriander	cilantro
corking	first rate
cornfield	wheat field
cornflour	cornstarch
Cornish pasty (see pasty)	pastry filled with meat, onions, potatoes and vegetables
cosh (see under the cosh)	blackjack, club
cosset	pamper or spoil
cossie (*abbr.* costume)	bathing suit, swimming suit
costermonger	street trader of fruit, fish, etc.

English	American
costers	hucksters
costume (*see* cossie)	bathing suit, swimming suit
cot	crib
cotch (*go ...*)	relax together
cote	shelter for animals
cotton	thread
cotton reel	spool
cotton wool	absorbent cotton
couldn't give a fig	don't give a damn
couldn't give two pins	couldn't care less
couldn't swing a cat in it	very small space or room
council estate (*see* council housing)	public housing
council housing (*see* council estate)	public housing
council tax	local property tax which partly funds government
counterfoil	check stub
counterpane	bedspread

English	American
county (*very ...*)	stylish appearance
county lady	stylish lady
county set	upper class
courgette	zucchini
course (*doing a ...*)	course of study (including several academic courses)
court list	docket
court shoe (*ladies*)	pump
cove (*decent ...*)	fellow, chap
cow gum	rubber cement
cow parsley	Queen Ann's lace
cow pat	cow pie
crack	pleasant conversation
cracked vessel	crazy
cracker	a fun loving person; attractive woman
crackers	crazy, mad
cracking	very good

English	American
cracking good innings (*cricket metaphor*)	good job
crackling (*nice bit of ...*)	attractive woman
cravat	neck cloth
cream (double)	heavy cream
cream (single)	light cream
cream cracker	soda cracker
cream off	taken the best of something
cream tea	includes heavy whipped or clotted cream to spread on warm scones with strawberry jam
crease up	double over with laughter
cricket (*that's not ...*)	fair
Crikey! (*see* Blimey! Gorblimey!)	expression of surprise such as Son-of-a-gun! or Gee whiz!
Crimbo	Christmas
crisps	potato chips
crock	decrepit old person, something worn out

English	American
crocked	injured, gimpy
cross (*don't be ...*)	angry
crossing sweeper	street cleaner
crumpet	flat soft cake eaten toasted
crumpet (*nice bit of ...*)	sex, sexually attractive woman
crusty bread	white bread with crisp crust
cry off	withdraw
cup of char	cup of tea
cupboard	closet
cuppa	cup of tea
currant bread	raisin bread
current account	checking account
curriculum vitae (*see c.v.*)	resumé
cut a dash	make a good impression
cut and thrust (*... ... ... situation*)	aggressively fighting for position
cut up (*car ... me ...*)	cut off

English	American
cutlery	silverware
cutlet	chop
cutting (*... from the Times*)	newspaper clipping
cuttings book	scrap book
c.v. (*abbr.* curriculum vitae)	resumé

D

dab hand	skillful
dabs	fingerprints
daft	stupid, silly
dame	a woman who has been awarded OBE or another order of chivalry
damp (*n.*) (*the ...*)	damp weather
dancing pumps	dancing shoes
dandle (*v.*)	bounce a child on one's knee
dashed (*I'll be ...*)	I'll be damned
daunting	formidable challenge, difficult task

English	American
davenport	small writing table with drawers
day tripper (*see tripper*)	person who goes on a one-day trip for pleasure
dead head (*v.*) (*... ... the roses*)	cut and remove dead growth (e.g. flowers)
deaf aid	hearing aid
dear	expensive
death duty	estate tax
death warmed up	death warmed over
dell	small wooded area
demerara sugar	brown sugar
dental surgery	dentist's office
deposit account	savings account
deputation	representative group
derry	a run-down derelict building
desiccated (*... coconut*)	dried
desk diary	date book

English	American
des res (*abbr.* desirable residence) (*see* nice address)	nice neighborhood
detached house	a single house not connected to another house
details (*your ...*)	personal information
devolution	separate legislatures for Wales and Scotland
diamanté	rhinestone
diamond (*he's a ... lad*)	good person
diary (*n.*) (*check my ...*)	calendar, schedule
diary up (*v.*)	make an appointment
dicky (*adv.*)	feeling under the weather, shaky, weak, defective
dicky (*n.*)	bow tie
dicky bird (*never heard a ... ... out of him*)	a peep, a word
did a bunk (*see* bunk off)	not show up for a commitment, a no-show
did a flip	took a trip
did a flit (*see* did a runner, doing a moonlight)	leave to evade debt or liability

English	American
did a runner (*see* did a flit, doing a moonlight)	ran away having taken money or not paid a debt
diddling (*How are ya diddlin'?*)	how are you doing, getting along
diet sheet	list of things to eat (or avoid) for medical or slimming purposes
digit	finger, toe
din-din	lunch or dinner (used by or for children)
ding dong	argument
dingle	small wooded area
dinky	small, cute or neat item
dinner jacket	tuxedo
directory enquiries (*telephone*)	directory assistance, information
dirty stop out	one who has stayed out late at night and partied
dirty weekend	weekend with friend, including sex
disenable (*... the machine*)	render inoperable
dishy	attractive (female)

English	American
disorderly house	brothel
Dispirin	soluble aspirin
disport (v.)	conduct oneself
distance learning	correspondence course
district (police)	precinct
dither (n.) (in a ...)	state of indecision
dither (v.) (to ...) (see faff, fuss)	engage in unnecessary, indecisive activity
dither about (v.) (see faff about, fuss about)	engage in unnecessary, indecisive activity
dithery (adj.)	indecisive
diversion	detour
divvy	foolish, idiotic
DIY store	store which sells paint, wallpaper, etc. for persons doing their own decorating (lit. do-it-yourself)
DIYers	people who do their own home decorating
do (n.)	party

English	American
do the dirty (... ... ... *on him*)	act which harms another person, to betray
dock	enclosed area in a courtroom where the accused sits or stands during trial
docker	longshoreman
doctor's surgery	doctor's office
dodder	move unsteadily
dodge the column	avoid one's obligation or duty
dodgy	suspect, untrustworthy
doggo	lie still (like a dog)
dog's body	one given a slavish job, gopher
dog's bollocks (*the ... ...*)	top notch, first rate
dog's breakfast (*make a ... ... of it*) (*see* pig's breakfast)	mess
dog's dinner (*looked like a ... ...*)	unattractive, messy

doing a moonlight

doing a moonlight (*see did a flit, did a runner*)	leave and avoid one's obligation (*e.g.* pay rent)
dole (*see on the dole*)	money received from the government, unemployment compensation
dollop	small amount

English	American
dolly-bird	nice looking young woman, more likely to be a bimbo
don	member of college or university faculty
done and dusted	completely finished
done one of them up	hitting someone
donkey's years	a long time
don't give a monkey's	couldn't care less
doppelganger	ghost
Dorset knob	hard, round cracker
dosh	money
doss house	flop house
dosser	tramp or layabout
dossing	sleeping on the floor, on a couch, etc.
dot (*since the year ...*)	for a very long time
dotty	batty, absurd
down at heel	in need of repair, run down
down market	lower priced

English	American
down pipe	down spout
down the pan	down the tubes
down tools (v.)	take a break, stop work
drag	(usually) scented object attached to a rope and used to attract dogs
dragging up	move up
drape	curtain
draper	one who deals in fabrics
draught excluder	weather stripping
draughts	checkers
draw even	meet at same spot, even with
draw up (v.)	come to a halt
draw up (v.) (... ... *a chair*)	pull up
drawing pin	thumbtack
dress circle	mezzanine
dressing gown	bathrobe or housecoat
drink driving	drunk driving

English	American
drink in (... ... an experience)	take in, appreciate
drinks party	cocktail party
driving license	driver's license
droll (very ...)	quaintly amusing
drop off the perch (see drop off the twig)	die
drop off the twig (see drop off the perch)	die
dross (see rubbish)	nonsense
drunk as a lord	very drunk, smashed
dry (in the ...)	dry place
dual carriageway (see carriageway)	divided highway, four-lane highway
dubbin	a substance rubbed on leather (ball or shoes) to keep it soft and waterproof
duck (cricket metaphor)	a score of nothing (batter bowled out without scoring a run)
duck ("Whatcha want ... ?")	term for person
duff (adj.) (a ... pen)	useless, worthless

English	American
duff (v.)	beat
duff up	to beat up someone
duffle coat	hooded overcoat
dull (*weather*)	overcast and cloudy
dullaly	going crazy
dummy	pacifier
dungarees	overalls
dust binned	thoroughly defeated
dust cart	truck which collects trash
dustbin (*see* wheely bin)	trash can, garbage can
duster	dry cleaning cloth
dustman (*see* binman)	garbage or trash collector
dust-up (*see* bust-up)	verbal confrontation, fight
duvet (*see* continental quilt)	comforter (used on top of a sheet in lieu of a blanket)
dynamo	generator

English	American

E

each way (*betting*)	bet to win, place or show
earl	British nobleman ranking next below marquess
early days (*it's ... ...*)	too soon to say
earn your crust	earn a living, make ends meet
earth (*electricity*)	ground wire
easy-peasy	very simple
eat like a gannet	eat like a horse
Edwardian	pertaining to the rein of King Edward VII (1901-1910)
eggs and chips	fried eggs and French fries
egg soldiers	bread squares dipped in soft-boiled egg
eggflip	eggnog
eiderdown	thin comforter (used on top of a sheet and blanket)
eisteddfod	Welsh festival with competition in music and other performing arts

English	American
elastic band	rubber band
elastoplast	band-aid

elastoplast

English	American
elephant trap	an obvious trap
elevenses (*n.*)	coffee break
Elizabethan	pertaining to the reign of Queen Elizabeth I (1558-1603)
embrocation	ointment (usually for aches and pains)
emery board	cardboard nail file
end of my tether	end of my rope
end of the day	when all is said and done, all things having been considered
engaged (*telephone*)	busy
engaged signal	busy signal

English	American
engagement diary	schedule, calendar
enquiries (*to make ...*)	investigate, look into
equerry	officer who acts as attendant to a member of a royal family
ER	Queen Elizabeth (*lit.* Elizabeth Regina)
escutcheon	shield with a coat of arms
escutcheon (*see* blot on your escutcheon)	honor, reputation
esplanade	public promenade
Essex girl (woman)	loose, vulgar female
estate agent	realtor
estate car	station wagon
evaporated milk	powdered milk
evensong	early evening church service (mainly prayers and singing)
ever so (*... ... kind*)	very
Exchequer	Department of Treasury
executive car	expensive, spacious car
eyewash	nonsense

English	American
face as long as a fiddle	look gloomy, miserable
face flannel (*see* flannel)	washcloth
factotum (*n.*) (*he is my ...*)	someone who does everything
faff (*v.*) (*to ...*) (*see* dither, fuss)	engage in unnecessary, indecisive activity
faff about (*v.*) (see dither about, fuss about)	engage in unnecessary, indecisive activity
fag	cigarette
fag (*see* fagmaster)	younger pupil who acts on instructions from older pupils in school
fag end	cigarette butt
fag hag	woman who hangs out with gay men
fagged out	tired, exhausted

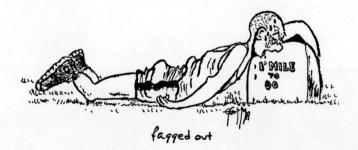

fagged out

English	American
faggot	meatball
faggots in gravy	meatballs in gravy
fagmaster (... *at Marlborough*) (*see* fag)	senior pupil who monitors fags' activities
fair crack of the whip	fair shake
fairly good nick (*see* nick)	fairly good physical condition
fairy cake	cupcake
fairy light	small colored decorative light, Christmas tree light
fall off your branch	fall asleep
fall out	have a disagreement, break off relations
fallen off the back of a lorry	stolen item
false dawn	false ray of hope
famously	done extremely well
fancy (*v.*)	like, be attracted to, want to do something
fancy oneself	have a high opinion of oneself
fancy woman	mistress

English	American
fanny	vagina
farrago	jumbled mixture of things, nonsense
Father Christmas	Santa Claus
FC	soccer club
fed to the back teeth	thoroughly fed up
fee note	bill
fell out off relations	had a disagreement, broke
felt (see roofing felt)	lining under shingle
fencer	fence, receiver and seller of stolen goods
fête	community or school sale with party atmosphere
fetching (she looks ...)	attractive
fettle (fine ...)	condition, shape (person)
fey (a bit ...)	effeminate
fiddle (... the figures) (see on the fiddle)	deceptive manipulation
fight your corner	speak up, make your case
filbert	hazelnut

English	American
fillip (give a ...)	boost
film	movie
fine point (not to put too ...a ... on it)	without exaggeration (usually ironic)
finger	shot of liquor
fingerstall	cover to protect an injured finger
fire brigade	fire department
fire raiser	arsonist
first degree (a first)	highest rank in British university degree classification system (roughly comparable to A grade in U.S.)
first floor	second floor
first instance (... ... judge)	trial court
first light	daybreak
first past the post (racing metaphor)	first to finish
first year (undergraduate)	freshman
firth	narrow inlet of the sea
fish fingers	fish sticks

English	American
fish knife	knife
fish slice	spatula
fishing float	bobber
fishing rod	fishing pole
fishmonger	one who sells fish
fishwife	scolding woman
fit out	provide with the necessary equipment
fit up	frame (for a crime)
fits and starts	done in disjointed, spasmodic manner
fitted carpet	wall-to-wall
fittings (*house*)	appliances
fiver	five pound note
fives	handball
fixture	athletic contest, game
flake out	pass out, faint
flan	quiche
flannel	exaggerated talk or flattery

English	American
flannel (*see* face flannel)	washcloth
flapdoodle	nonsense
flash-Harry	loudly dressed and obnoxious man
flat	apartment
flat cap (see cloth cap)	reference to working class person, particularly a trade union member
flatmate	roommate
fleapit	dingy, seedy place
Fleet Street (*... ... reporters*)	newspaper
flex	electric cord, wire
flibbertigibbet	flighty person, usually female
flick knife	switchblade
flick of a lamb's tail	in a second
flip through	look at a book or magazine quickly
flip-flops	rubber-soled sandals, floppers
flippin' (*adj.*) (*you ... idiot*)	euphemism for fucking, frigging

English	American
flitch	piece of bacon
float (*see* fishing float) (*n.*)	bobber
flogged off	sold
floor walker (*see* shop assistant)	sales clerk
flotation	an organization converted into a publicly quoted company
flotsam and jetsam	odds and ends
fluff (*bit of ..., piece of ...*)	mistress
fluff (*n.*)	mistake
fluff (*v.*)	make a mistake
flume	channel or water slide
flummox	bewilder, perplex
fly	cunning, crafty
fly boy (*see* wide boy)	crafty, devious person
fly leaf	blank page at the beginning or end of a book
fly poster	poster on a wall

English	American
fly tipping	illegal dumping
flying fox	fruit-eating bat
fly-over	overpass
fob off	keep one at bay by giving a person something not good or not wanted
foolscap	legal size paper
football	soccer
football manager	soccer coach
footbridge	bridge for pedestrians
footman	male servant in uniform
footpath (see pavement)	sidewalk, walkway, lane
footway	sidewalk next to bridge
forecourt	paved area in front of a building
form	one year of secondary school, grade
form mistress	female schoolteacher
fortnight	two weeks
forty winks	brief sleep, nap

English	American
foul (*v.*) (*... the footpath*)	soil
foul (v.) (*ship will ... the ocean floor*)	strike
fourth year (*undergraduate*)	senior
free house	pub not owned by a particular brewery
French beans	string beans
French letter	condom
Frenchie	condom
fresh (*... information*)	new, newly discovered
fresher (*university*)	freshman
fretwork	cut out intricate designs of wood or metal
Friday car	a car that has frequent mechanical problems, a lemon
fried slice	fried bread (in oil or lard)
frightfully	very great, extremely
fringe (*hair*)	bangs
frippet	frivolous young woman

English	American
frog	French person
frog march	forced escort
from the off	from the beginning
front bench	parliamentary leaders of the government or opposition
front door is open	unzipped, fly is open
frowsy	disheveled, untidy
frying pan	skillet
fry-up	fried breakfast
fuddled	confused
fug	hot and stuffy
full as an egg	completely full
full of himself	conceited, pompous, self-centered
full on	all the way
full shilling (*not the ... ...*)	not very intelligent
full stop (*punctuation*)	period

English	American
fullness of time (*in the ... ...*)	in due course (the implication is don't hold your breath)
funfair	fair
funnily enough	oddly enough, interestingly enough
funny bone	crazy bone
fusilier	soldier of certain regiments
fuss (*v.*) (*to ...*) (*see* dither, faff)	engage in unnecessary, indecisive activity
fuss about (*v.*) (*see* dither about, faff about)	engage in unnecessary, indecisive activity
fusspot	fussy, complaining person

G

English	American
gabble	rapid indistinct speech, chatter
gaff	house, home
gaffer	person in charge
gallery	balcony
game (*on the ...*)	working as a prostitute

English	American
game not worth the candle	not worth it
"Game on!"	begin playing a game
game pie	cooked pheasant, hare or venison in a pastry crust
gammon	ham
gangway	aisle
gannet	a greedy person
gaol	jail
gap (see mind the gap)	space between train and platform
gap year	one year period before attending university
garden (back ..., front ...)	yard, lawn
garden party	lawn party
garret	attic room
gasbag	person who talks too much, windbag
gasholder	large tank for holding gas
gassing (... away)	talking

English	American
gastropub	pub which serves a wide range of food selections (resembles a restaurant)
gateaux	cake
gaudy	college alumni party
gave a fright	scared
gay deceivers	falsies

gay deceivers

English	American
gazump (*real estate*)	back out of agreement to take a better offer
gazunder (*real estate*)	back out of agreement and demand a lower price
GCH	gas-fired central heating
GCSE	General Certificate of Secondary Education, examinations usually taken at age fifteen or sixteen
gear lever	gearshift
gearbox (*motor car*)	transmission (automobile)
gen (*n.*)	information
gen up (*v.*)	study, become informed
general	family doctor
genned up	well informed
gentleman	formerly a descriptive term for a man of nobility; in modern usage it refers to an upper class person or a well mannered person
gents	men's restroom or bathroom
Geordie	person from Newcastle upon Tyne

English	American
get his end away (see get his leg-over)	have sex with a woman, get laid
get his leg-over (see leg-over, get his end away)	have sex with a woman, get laid
get my head around	try to understand
get on (... ... with)	get along
get on the game	go into prostitution
get on to (... ... ... him) (see chase up)	contact a person (and usually insist that something be done)
get one's leg over (see leg-over)	have sex with a woman, get laid
get out (a ... ...)	way out
get stuffed	get lost, go away
get the bullet (see get the push, get your cards, sack)	get fired
get the push (see get the bullet, get your cards, sack)	get fired
get weaving	get on with it, get going
get your cards (see get the bullet, get the push, sack)	get fired
getting to grips	coming to grips

English	American
geyser	water heater
gimcrack	of poor quality, cheaply made
gimp	courage, guts
gin palace	expensive motorized boat
giro cheque	government benefit check
git (*looney old ...*)	old person (derogatory)
give a bell (*... me ... ...*)	call on the telephone
give evidence	testify in a legal proceeding
give it a miss	skip, don't do or pursue something
give over	shut up, stop doing something
give the game away (*see* blow the gaff)	divulge a secret
give the slip	evade, escape
give way	yield
given to understand	informed
glacé fruits	candied fruits

English	American
glad rags	best clothes
Glasgow kiss	head-butt
glory hole	spare room
glowworm	lightning bug
gnat's piss	weak beverage
go (*give it a ...*)	try, make an effort, give it a shot
go cotch	relax
go down (*jail*)	sentenced to period in jail
go off	become stale or rotten
Go on!	You're kidding!
go through (*sport*)	advance
go to law	initiate formal legal proceedings
gob	mouth
gobbet	lump of food
gobsmacked	shocked, surprised and speechless
gobstopper (*sweet*)	jawbreaker (candy)

God-box

God-box	church
goggle box (*see* box)	television
going over	past its peak
going to see a man about a dog	leaving for a short time without giving a reason, usually to use the bathroom
gone down (*college student*)	gone home for vacation
gone missing (*he's ... ...*)	disappeared
gone over	wilted or died
gone to ground	in hiding (derived from fox hunting)

English	American
gone to the wall	ended, gone out of business, declared bankruptcy
gone up (*college student*)	gone back to school
gongs (*see* knighthood)	honors (e.g. annual honors and medals given by the Queen)
good form	proper way something is done
good form (*person*)	good condition
good innings (*cricket metaphor*) (*he's had a ... ...*)	good life, usually an elderly person
good news (*he's ... ...*)	good person
good nick	good condition
goods wagon	freight car
googly	cricket ball which changes direction unexpectedly on the bounce
goose pimples	goose bumps

gooseberry

gooseberry	unwanted chaperone
Gorblimey! (see Blimey! Crikey!)	expression of surprise such as Son-of-a-gun! or Gee whiz!
gorgon	ugly person
gormless	stupid
got (have ... it right)	gotten
got at (been ... ...)	persuaded, manipulated
governor (prison ...)	warden
graft (n.)	hard work
graft (v.)	work hard

English	American
grafter (*n.*)	hard worker
grammar school	school for children between ages eleven and eighteen where admission is based upon academic ability
granny, grannie	grandma, grandmother
grant (*education*)	scholarship
grasp the nettle	deal with a difficult issue
grass (*n.*)	person who informs (especially on criminals)
grass (*v.*)	betray a confidence by revealing information
grass widow	wife whose husband is absent for a time
greaseproof paper	wax paper
green (*village ...*)	public grassy area
green (*end of the ...*)	grass area on which bowls is played
green fingers	green thumb
green goddess	army truck used when fire fighters are on strike

English	American
green grocer	shop which sells vegetables and fruit only
green man	walk signal at pedestrian crossing
green pepper (see red pepper)	bell pepper
green welly brigade	disparaging description of upper class people in the countryside
greens	vegetables
gricer	person interested in trains
gridiron	football
griff (n.)	a tip
griffin (n.)	a tip
grill (v.)	broil
grip wood (see touch wood)	knock on wood, hopeful
grist to one's mill	something that benefits oneself
grit	sand
grit box	container for sand used on icy road

English	American
gritter (see gritter lorry, gritting vehicle)	truck which spreads a mixture of salt and sand on snowy and icy roads
gritter lorry (see gritter, gritting vehicle)	truck which spreads a mixture of salt and sand on snowy and icy roads
gritting vehicle (see gritter, gritter lorry)	truck which spreads a mixture of salt and sand on snowy and icy roads
grizzle (v.)	whine or complain
grizzling	complaining
grizzly	complaining
grotty (I feel ...)	rotten, bad
grousing	moaning, whining, complaining
grumble guts	complaining person
guard (railway)	conductor
gudgeon pin (automotive)	wrist pin (connects piston to connecting rod)
guillotine coming down	time is up
guinea	one pound and one shilling (five pence)

English	American
gumboots (see Wellies)	waterproof rubber boots (below knee)
gun dog	hunting dog (usually birds)
gunge	sticky, messy substance
guppie	homosexual yuppie
gutted (*totally ...*)	devastated
guttering	eaves trough
guttersnipe	neglected slum child
guvner (*guv*)	supervisor, boss
Guy Fawkes Day	November 5, commemorates the Gunpowder Plot to blow up Parliament in 1605, during reign of James I
guzzle guts	greedy person
gyro check	government benefit check

H

hack	writer or journalist of mediocre ability
hacked off	fed up

English	American
hackwork	dull, repetitive work
haft	wooden handle (*e.g.* axe handle)
hair grip	bobby pin
hair shirt (*you bet your ... ...*)	to impose discomfort on oneself out of religious conviction, be a martyr
hair slide (*see* slide)	barrette
hairpin bend	hairpin curve or turn
half (*... seven*) (*see* half past)	thirty minutes past the hour (seven-thirty)
half-arsed	half-assed
half-holiday (schools)	half-day vacation
half-past (*see* half)	thirty minutes past the hour
ham salad	piece of ham with fresh vegetables
ham-handed	clumsy
hammer and tongs	with great effort or energy (*e.g.* verbal argument)
hammer to crack a nut (*to use a ... ...*)	too much, more than is required
handbag (*n.*)	purse

English	American
handbag (v.) (to ...)	woman treating a person or idea ruthlessly or insensitively
handle	official title (Sir, Lady)
handover	job training
hang about (don't ... ...)	delay, waste time
hangdog expression	sullen
happy as a Larry	happy as a lark, very happy
happy as a sandboy	happy as a lark, very happy
happy clapper	holy roller, fundamentalist Christian who engages in demonstrative behavior
happy pill	tranquilizer
hard ask	challenge
hard cheese	tough luck
hard graft	hard work
hard shoulder (road)	soft shoulder
harridan	shrew
hash (n.) (make a ... of)	mess

English	American
hash key (keyboard)	pound key
haulage	goods transported by truck or the charge for conveyance
haulier	one who hauls (e.g. a trucking company)
have a go	go ahead, proceed, do something
have it off	have sexual intercourse
having on (... *me* ...)	putting on, joking, kidding
hawk (*v.*)	sell door-to-door
hawker (*n.*)	one who sells door-to-door
head teacher (*see* headmaster)	principal (who may also teach)
headlamp	headlight
headmaster (*see* head teacher)	principal
Hear! Hear!	exclamation of approval or agreement
heath	bog land
Heath Robinson (*made a ... ... job of it*)	poor quality but works

English	American
heather	shrub with small flower growing on hills and mountains
heaven on a stick	just what is needed, first rate
heaving	packed with people
heavy going	difficult
heck as like	absolutely not
herbert	fool or stupid person
het up	worked up
hiding (a ...)	whipping, thrashing
hiding to nothing	despite one's best efforts one won't succeed, beating your head against a brick wall
higgledy-piggledy	in confusion

high camp

English	American
high camp (*see* camp)	ostentatiously gay
high street	main street
high table (*see* top table)	head table in dining hall of a (usually) Cambridge or Oxford college

English	American
high tea	served around 6:00 p.m., as a light supper, includes an entrée (such as chicken a la King or meat pie), along with breads, salad, cheese, fruit and dessert
Highness	title used to address or refer to a royal person
hire	rent
hire-purchase (see never-never)	installment plan
hit for six (cricket metaphor)	devastated, overcome emotionally
hive(d) off	separate(d) from a group
HM	Her (or His) Majesty
hoardings	billboards
hoarfrost	white ground frost
hob	flat top part of a stove
hobble de hoy	clumsy, immature young male
hockey	field hockey
hoi polloi	ordinary people
hoick	raise abruptly

English	American
hoity-toity	arrogant, haughty
hold tight	hold the bar in a bus
holdall	large soft canvas or leather bag
holiday (*see* hols)	vacation
hols (*abbr.* holiday)	vacation
home bird	homebody
homely	comfortable, cozy
Honours List	list of honors (e.g. knighthood, C.B.E., O.B.E.) awarded by The Queen twice a year
hooray Henry	bone-headed, loud public school man

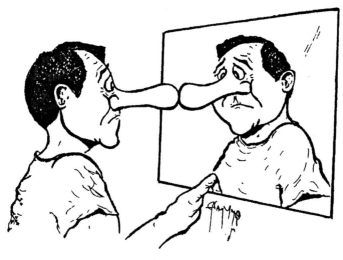

hooter

hooter	nose
Hoover (*n.*)	vacuum cleaner
Hoover (*v.*)	to vacuum
hopping mad	extremely annoyed
horse falls at the first fence	idea or proposal going nowhere
horses for courses	the right person for the job
hose pipe	garden hose
hotelier	hotel manager, owner
hothouse (*parents ... children*)	provide extra tutoring

English	American
hotter (*n.*)	one who engages in joyriding
hotting (*v.*)	joyriding, young people speeding in "hot" cars on public roads
hotting up (*competition is … …*)	becoming intense
housebound	shut-in
householder	homeowner
housing estate	subdivision
howler	stupid mistake
how's your father (*a bit of … … …*)	sex with a woman, nooky
hoyden	boisterous girl
HRH	Her (or His) Royal Highness
huge sweep of things	grand scheme of things
hugger muggering	behind the scenes maneuvering, scheming
hull (*v.*)	shuck
hump (*n.*) (*speed …*)	speed bump
hump (*v.*)	lift or carry

English	American
hundreds and thousands	sprinkles (candy, cookie)
hurling (*see* spew)	vomiting, throwing-up
hustings (*on the ...*)	campaigning for election
Hyacinth Bucket (*she's a ... ...*)	social climbing with snobbery

I

ice (*see* sorbet)	sherbet
ice cream cornet	ice cream cone
ice(d) lolly	popsicle
ice hockey	hockey
icing	frosting
icing sugar	powdered sugar
identification parade	lineup
identikit	a group of pictures of parts of faces that can be combined to form a likeness of a police suspect
immersion heater	water heater
in (*sun went ...*)	down

English	American
in a state	in a bad mood, agitated
in hospital	in the hospital
in post	on the job, working
in service	employed in private home
in the buff	naked
in the club (*see banged up, preg, preggy, preggers, up the duff*)	pregnant

in the club

English	American
in the frame	suspect in a criminal investigation; being considered for an appointment
in the nick (*see* nick)	in jail
in the post	in the mail
in the round	taking all things into consideration
in the Scrubs	in prison (Wormwood Scrubs)
in the street (*live ... ...*)	on the street
in the wars	in pain
in tray (*see* out tray)	in box
independent school	private school
indicator (*see* winker)	turn signal on a car
industrial action	strike
infra dig (*adj.*)	beneath one's dignity
Inland Revenue	Internal Revenue Service
inquiry	official investigation
inside	in jail

English	American
insolvency	bankruptcy
inter-city	fast traveling transportation service between cities
Inverness cape	type of cape which Sherlock Holmes is often depicted as wearing
inverted commas	quotation marks, quotes
invigilator	proctor, supervisor of an examination
ironmonger	hardware store

J

jab	shot, injection

jab

English	American
jack it in	throw in the towel
jacket potato	baked potato
Jacobean	of the reign of King James I of England
Jacobite	supporter of the Stuarts after the overthrow of King James II of England
jam	jelly
jam for tea	a treat, something extra
jammy	very lucky
jammy devil (see jammy dodger)	lucky person
jammy dodger (see jammy devil)	lucky person
Janet and John (... ... ... bit)	basic information or instruction on a subject
jape	prank, joke
jar	glass of beer
jelly	jello
jerkin	sleeveless jacket
jerry	a German

English	American
jerry can	gas can
jerry-built	poorly built
jersey	pullover, sweater
jib at	object to
jiggery pokery	skullduggery, trickery
jim jams (*give me the ... ...*)	willies, heeby jeebies
jimmy riddle (*see* piddle, slash, tiddle, widdle)	urinate

jimmy riddle

English	American
job lot	miscellaneous items sold together, collection of items of low value
job seeker's allowance	government payment to one who seeks employment
jobbery (*n.*)	corrupt practice
jobsworth	over-zealous official
jocose	humorous, playful
Joe Bloggs (*see Joe Soap, Man on the Clapham Omnibus*)	Joe Blow, hypothetical average person, ordinary man in the street
Joe Soap (*see Joe Bloggs, Man on the Clapham Omnibus*)	Joe Blow, hypothetical average person, ordinary man in the street
johnny	condom
joined up (*... ... government*)	coordinated policy between departments
joiner	cabinet maker
joint (*meat*)	a roast
jolly (*... well played*) (*see jolly good*)	very
jolly good (*see jolly*)	very good

English	American
jot (*care not a ...*)	bit, in the least, at all
jotter (*old ...*)	codger
journo	journalist
joy-house	brothel
joystick	control device for airplane or computer
joystick	penis
jug	pitcher
juggernaut	large semi-truck
jump leads	jumper cables
jump the queue	not wait one's turn in line, cut in line
jumper	sweater
junior	assistant
junker	dealer in stolen cars

English	American
K	

kecks — pants, trousers

kedgeree — breakfast dish including fish, rice and hard-boiled eggs

keen — eager, enthusiastic

kerfuffle (*What a ...!*) — commotion, disorder

key deposit — deposit for keys required by some real estate agents when they accompany you to view property

kick him up in the air — kick in the rear, to rouse another

kick into touch (*rugby metaphor*) — eliminate a problem

kick over the traces — break loose

kick up (*... ... a fuss*) — create confusion, complain

kiddywink — young child

kidney pudding (*abbr.* steak and kidney pie) — chunks of beef and lamb kidney in gravy with pastry crust

kill speed (*... your ...*) — slow down (car)

kine — pig

kiosk — booth where tickets, newspapers, etc. are sold; public telephone booth

Kiosk

kip — brothel

kip — nap

kippered — fooled, taken for a ride

kippers — smoked herring

English	American
kiss of life	mouth-to-mouth resuscitation
kit (*see* clobber)	clothing
kit bag	bag for personal belongings, gym bag
kit out (*see* kitted)	provide clothes or equipment for a particular occasion
kitch	in bad taste, tacky
kitchen garden	garden for growing vegetables, herbs, etc.
kite-mark	official designation of approval, certification
kite-marking (*system of ... ...*)	quality control process by which items are officially approved
kith and kin	family
kitman	equipment manager
kitted (*see* kit out)	provide clothes or equipment for a particular occasion
knackered	exhausted
knacker's yard	place where old horses were taken for slaughter

English	American
knees-up (*n.*)	party with dancing, gig
knee-trembler	sexual intercourse while standing up
knickers (*female*)	underpants, panties
knickers in a twist	confused and worked up about something
knighthood (*see* gongs)	high honor given annually by the Queen
knob	penis
knob	small portion
knobs on (*with ... ...*)	to emphasize
knock about	roughhousing
knock back (*v.*) (*... ... a few*)	have a few drinks
knock back (*had a ... ...*)	disappointment
knock down (*see* pull down)	tear down, demolish
knock down prices	reduced
knock(ed) for six (*cricket metaphor*) (*see* hit for six)	devastated, overcome emotionally
knock it on the head	stop doing something (*e.g.* stop smoking)

English	American
knock-on effect (*rugby metaphor*)	ripple effect
knock over	run down (car)
knock up	call, wake up, knock on the door
knock up (*tennis*)	warm up
knocking shop	brothel, house of prostitution
knowledge (*the ...*)	information learned to become a licensed London taxi driver

L

English	American
label	tag
lackwit	witless or stupid person, nitwit
lad	boy, guy
ladette	young woman who drinks and swears (like the lads)
Lady Muck (*see Lord Muck*)	pompous, opinionated woman
ladybird	ladybug

English	American
lady-in-waiting	female servant of queen or princess
lag	convict
lager lout	young man who drinks lager and is obnoxious
Lancashire Hotpot	lamb and vegetable casserole
landlubber	person who is not experienced at sea
larder	pantry, storeroom
lark about	play jokes, pranks
lashings	lots of
laughing like a drain	laughing loudly, howling with laughter
laundromat	money launderer
lavatory	bathroom, restroom, john
law court	court
lay the table	set the table
layabout	lazy person, loafer
lay-by	rest stop

English	American
lead in the pencil	male sexual potency
leader	editorial (newspaper)
league tables	formerly a list of standings of football teams within their divisions; more recently a list of ratings
learnt	learned
lecky man (*see* spark)	electrician
legless	very drunk
leg-over (*n.*) (*see* get his leg-over, get his end away)	have sex with a woman, get laid

leg-over

English	American
let	rent, lease
letterbox (*see pillarbox*)	mailbox on the street; however, the upright cylindrical ones are more traditionally called pillarboxes; slot in a door through which letters are delivered
level (*sport*)	tie score, tied, even
level pegging	even, equal footing
liaise	contact, meet another person
lickspittle	sycophant, toady, brown-nose
lie-down (*a ... ...*)	sexual intercourse
lie-in	long stay in bed in the morning
life coach	counselor
lift	elevator
ligger (*n.*)	freeloader
like a bomb (*went ... ...*)	success, a hit
like it or lump it	take it or leave it

English	American
limited company	incorporated (private)
limpbound book	paperback book
linctus	cough medicine
lip-gloss	lipstick
liquidizer	blender
liver sausage	liverwurst
loaf (*use your ...*)	brain, common sense
local (*the ...*)	neighborhood bar
local authority	governing body of a county or district
lodger	roomer
lollipop man/lady	crossing guard
lolly	lollipop
lolly	money
lone parent	single parent
long view (*take the ... ...*)	plan ahead
loo	toilet with or without a wash basin
loo roll	toilet paper

English	American
look see (*have a ... ...*)	look around
look up	check out
lord	peer of realm; Lord prefix as designation of certain ranks of peerage
Lord love a duck!	expression of surprise
Lord Lucan (*done a ... ...*)	disappear, vanish
Lord Muck (*see* Lady Muck)	pompous, opinionated man
lordship	title used in addressing or referring to a man with a rank of Lord
lorry	truck
lorry (*open-back*)	pick-up truck
lorry driver	trucker
lose your rag	lose your temper
lost property	lost and found
lost the plot	unaware, lack of insight
lot (*the whole ...*)	amount
lot (*you ...*)	people

English	American
loudhailer	bullhorn
lounge	living room
lounge suit	business suit
love (*thanks ...*)	darling, honey
love bite (*on neck*)	hickey
lovely	very good
love-up	holding and caressing another
lower second degree (2.2)	third highest rank in British university degree classification system (roughly comparable to B-/C+ grade in U.S.)
lucky dip	grab bag
lug	ear
lump	awkward or stupid person

M

mack (*abbr.* mackintosh)	raincoat
mackintosh, (*see* mack)	raincoat

English	American
madam	spoiled or conceited girl
madden	mound, high place
made to measure (*clothing*)	custom made
made up	delighted, happy
magistrate	justice of the peace, lay judge
mailshot	mailing, circular
maisonette	flat on two floors
maize	corn
make a balls of	ruin, screw up
make a go of	be successful
make a hash of	mess up, screw up, ruin
make a meal of	make a big deal out of something
make a move	go
Makum	person from Sunderland
Man on the Clapham Omnibus (see Joe Bloggs, Joe Soap)	hypothetical average person, ordinary man in the street

English	American
manager (*see* football manager)	coach
mangetout	snow peas
manifesto (*political*)	platform
manky	horrid, second rate
manor	district, police precinct
marge (*abbr.* margarine)	margarine, oleo
mark (*n.*)	student's grade
mark (*v.*)	grade student's examination paper
mark (*v.*) (*... your man*)	guard your opponent in a sporting event
mark your card	got your number
market garden	place where fruit and vegetables are grown for sale
market town	town with designated area where farmers bring produce to sell
Marks and Sparks	Marks and Spencer
Marmite soldiers (*see* soldiers)	salty black vegetable spread on bread fingers

English	American
marque (car)	brand, make
marrow	squash
mash (see bangers and mash)	mashed potatoes
mash (v.)	brew tea
mate	male friend
maths	math, mathematics
matted (see carpeted)	disciplined
mature student (university)	older student
Maundy Thursday	Thursday before Easter when the Queen distributes Maundy money to people who have done charitable deeds
mawkish	foolishly sentimental
MBE	Member of the Order of the British Empire
meat pie	cooked meat with pastry crust
medical (a ...)	physical, physical examination
meet (Boxing Day ...)	a hunt with riders and hounds

English	American
mess about (*see* muck about)	mess around
methylated spirits	denatured alcohol
mews	street or paved area (originally stables)
mews house	a converted carriage house
mick	Irish person
mickey (*take the ... out of*) (*see* take the piss)	tease or kid another person
mickey (*to do a ...*)	to leave quickly
midden (*n.*) (*see* rubbish tip, tip)	trash dump
middling	so-so
mileometer	odometer
milk float	electrical vehicle used for delivery of milk and dairy products (formerly horse drawn)
milksop (*n.*)	weak, ineffectual person
mince	ground meat
minced (*meat*)	ground

English	American
mincer	meat grinder
mind (*... your head*)	beware of, watch for
mind the gap (*see gap*)	watch out for the space between the train and the platform
minder (*child*)	babysitter
minerals	soft drinks
minging	ugly
mingy	miserly
minicab	unlicensed, unmarked cab
minister (*... of the Crown*)	head of government department
minx (*n.*)	scheming woman
mix (*in a ...*)	muddle, mess
mohican (hairstyle)	mohawk
moke	donkey
moll	gangster's girl
mollock	engage in sexual intercourse

English	American
momentarily	lasting for a moment, just a second
money for old rope	money for nothing
monkey nut	peanut
monopoly man (*see* cobbler, slusher)	counterfeiter
mooch (*... around*)	kill time
moot (*n.*) (*the ...*)	debate
moot (*v.*)	debate
moppet	child
morning suit	matching coat with tails and pants, gray vest and tie
m.o.t. (*current ...*)	permit or certificate of roadworthiness for car or truck
Mothering Sunday	traditional name for Mother's Day, part of church calendar with date fixed by reference to Easter
Mother's ruin	gin
motor (*n.*)	automobile, car

English	American
motor (*v.*)	drive, take a trip
motor car	automobile, car
motoring offense	traffic violation
motorway	freeway, four-lane highway, interstate highway
mouth organ	harmonica
movements (*my ... for tomorrow*)	activities, schedule
muck about (*see mess about*)	mess around
muck in (*didn't ... ...*)	fit in
muck up	muddle, screw up
mucker(s) (*she and I were ...*)	friend(s)
mudguard	fender
muesli	granola
mug	fool
muggins	stupid or gullible person
mugs off (*darts*)	loser goes first
mum	mom, mother

English	American
mummy	mommy
mumping (*n.*)	accepting by police of bribe

mumping

mushy peas	dried peas boiled and mashed
muslin	cheesecloth

mutton dressed up as lamb

mutton dressed up as lamb	older person trying to appear youthful (e.g. middle-aged woman wearing a mini-skirt)
muzzy	confused

English	American
N	
naff	out of style
naff off (*v.*)	go away, fuck off
nail varnish	nail polish
nana (*bit of a ...*) (see clot)	idiot
nancy	male homosexual
nanny state	welfare state (pejorative overtone)
napper	head
nappy	diaper
nark (*n.*)	an informant
nark (*n.*)	one who complains in an irritating manner
nark (*v.*)	annoy
narky	complaining
narrow squeak	narrow escape
national service (*see* conscription)	specialized military draft limited to two years
natter (*n.*)	a chat, conversation

English	American
natter (*v.*)	have a chat
nattering	talking too long
natty	sharp, neat
naught (*see* nought)	nothing, figure 0
naughties	nooky
navvy	manual laborer

navvy

English	American
nay (see *née*)	indicating the maiden name of a married woman
near-side lane	lane closest to shoulder
near the knuckle	approaching indecency, improper behavior
neat (*drink*) (*I'll have it ...*)	straight
neck (*get it in the ...*)	take it in the ear
née (see nay)	indicating the maiden name of a married woman
nerve oneself	prepare to do something difficult or unpleasant, psyche-up
net curtains	sheer curtains, sheers
netball	team game in which a ball is thrown through a net hanging from a rim atop a pole (similar to basketball but with no backboard)
never-never (*see* hire-purchase)	installment purchase
newsagent	store which sells newspapers and magazines
newsreader	newscaster

English	American
NGO	non-governmental organization
NHS	National Health Service
nice address (*that's a ... ...*) (*see* des res)	nice area or neighborhood
nice as pie	nice as can be, very nice
nick (*in good ...*)	physical condition
nick (*n.*)(*see* in the nick)	police station, jail
nick (*v.*)	arrest
nick (*v.*)	steal
nicky noos (*see* odds and sods)	odds and ends
niffy (*see* whiffy, pong)	bad smelling
niggle	ache or pain; small worry or doubt
niggly	irritable
night of the long knives	firing of several members of an organization
nig-nog	foolish person
nil	zero

English	American
ninepins	bowling
nineteen to the dozen (*talks ... ...*)	fast
nip	hurry
nip	Japanese person
nipper	small child
no names no pack drill (*military*)	correct something done without revealing the culprit's name and there will be no punishment
nob (*see* toff)	big shot, important person
nobble (*v.*)	tamper with a racehorse, impair performance, to influence dishonestly
nobble (*v.*) (*racing metaphor*)	pressure someone to slow down, reduce criticism
noddle	head
Noddy car	a very small car (derogatory) after Enid Blyton's children's book character, Noddy
noddy dog	looking down when speaking
no-go (*... ... area*)	off limits

English	American
nonce	prisoner convicted of a sexual offense
non-starter	someone without a chance
non-U (see U)	non-acceptable by upper class, socially not acceptable
Norfolk jacket	outdoor sporting jacket (usually tweed)
Norman	pertaining to Normans (from Normandy, France), who conquered Saxon England in the Eleventh Century or their medieval architecture
nose out of joint	annoyed, upset
nosh (n.)	food
nosh (v.)	eat
noshery	restaurant
nosh-up	large serving of food
not a bad innings (cricket metaphor)	a good life
not a squeak	not a sound

English	American
not on (*see* off)	not the correct thing to do or say
not quite the ticket	not feeling well, not quite right
not slow in coming forward	pushy
note (*bank*)	bill
notice (*handed in my ...*)	resignation, quit
notice (*take ...*)	pay attention
notice board	bulletin board
notices (*theatre*)	critical reviews
nought (*see* naught)	nothing, figure 0
noughts and crosses	tic-tac-toe, X's and O's

noughts and crosses

English	American
now and again	occasionally, now and then
nub	the main point in a discussion
nuddy	nude
number plate	license plate
nutter (*he's a ...*)	crazy person, nut

O

OAP	old age pension or pensioner
OBE	Officer of the Order of the British Empire
ockey (*toe the ...*)	line from which darts are thrown
odd (*adj.*)	occasional
oddments	things left over
odds and sods (*see* nicky noos)	odds and ends
off (*from the ...*)	start, beginning, outset

English	American
off (*see* not on)	not the correct thing to do or say
off hand (*a bit ... ...*)	ungracious
off his head	crazy, foolish, off his rocker
off his own bat (*cricket metaphor*)	on his own
off license	liquor store
off pat (*learned his lines ... ...*)	perfectly
off peak (*... ... fare*)	cheaper rate
off peak (*... ... time*)	less busy time
off putting	disappointing, unwelcoming
off side lane	lane closest to median
off the boil	calmed down
off the boil (*a bit ... ...*)	not at peak performance, flat
off the peg clothes	ready to wear, not tailor-made
off the rails	break the rules
off your trolley	off your rocker

English	American
offcut	leftover piece
Oh my giddy aunt!	Oh my gosh!
OHMS	On Her/His Majesty's Service
Oi!	Hey you!
oik (see yob, yobbo)	aggressive, bad-mannered young person
old bill (see bill)	the police

old bill

English	American
old boy net	friends from private school
old boys	alumni
old crock	ailing old person
old lag	someone who has been around a long time; an habitual criminal
old man	male reference to male friend or acquaintance
Old Nick	the Devil
old sausage	dear friend
old school tie	system of mutual help and loyalty among former pupils of a private school
old stick (*dear ... ...*)	likeable elderly person
omnibus	bus
on (*have ...*)	planned
on about (*What are you ... ...?*)	talking about, saying
on appro	on approval
on his day	on a good day
on my baby's head	on the soul of my child

English	American
on offer	available
on rollerskates (... *his* ...)	very busy
on song	at your best
on the back foot (*cricket metaphor*)	in a difficult position
on the cards	in the cards
on the dole (*see* dole)	receiving public assistance
on the door	at the door
on the fiddle (*got it ... ...*) (*see* fiddle)	by deception (usually money)
on the hop (*caught ... ...*)	by surprise, unaware
on the job	sexual intercourse
on the mark	the exact point (discussion or subject)
on the nail	promptly (payment)
on the sick	drawing public assistance due to illness
once off	one time only
one and nine (*abbr.* one and nine pennies)	small amount of money (approximately one dime)

English	American
one off	one of a kind, not a regular happening
op (*medical*)	operation

OPC	out of parent's control, juvenile delinquent
open-back lorry	pick-up truck
open goal (*football metaphor*)	clear opportunity
open sewer	despicable person
open-hearted	big-hearted, generous
opposite	on the other side, across the street

English	American
opposite number	counterpart
other (*n.*) (*a bit of the ...*) (*see* rumpy-pumpy)	hanky panky
out on the tiles	out on the town
out tray (*see* in tray)	out box
outgoings	household expenses, utilities, etc.
oval	cricket ground
oven cloth (*see* oven glove)	pot holder
oven glove (*see* oven cloth)	pot holder
over egging the pudding (*see* over the top)	too much, undeserved
over the moon	overjoyed, happy
over the top (*OTT*) (*see* over egging the pudding)	too much, excessive
overleaf	reverse side of page
overspill (*n.*)	rehousing of people from crowded cities to smaller towns
overtake (*in car*)	pass

English	American
own goal (*football metaphor*)	something stupid
Oxbridge	Oxford and Cambridge Universities
Oxo cube	bouillon cube

P

P45	pink slip
pace	speed
pack (*cards*)	deck
pack (*papers*)	packet
packed out	full
packed up	closed
packet	large sum of money
paddock	field, pasture
Paddy	nickname for Irish person
paddy	fit of temper
pan(ned) (*v.*) (*... him*)	hit

English	American
panda car	police patrol car, a black and white
panel beater	a person who repairs damage to car bodies
pantechnicon	moving van
pantomime	dramatic (usually Christmas) entertainment based on a fairy-tale; dumb show (e.g. with males dressing as females, etc.)
pants	underwear
pap	nipple
paper knife	letter opener
paraffin	kerosene
paraffin lamp	kerosene lamp
paraffin wax	paraffin
parcel	package
parentheses (*see* round brackets)	parentheses
park and ride	parking lot on edge of town with transportation to downtown provided

English	American
parky	chilly
part (*take something in good ...*)	respond to statement (*e.g.* criticism) with good humor, having a good attitude
pass (*n.*)	lowest rank in British university degree classification system
pass degree	basic university qualification
pass over (*see* across the river)	die
pass the parcel	pass the buck (actually a small children's game in which a prize is wrapped in many layers of paper; sitting in a circle, the children pass it from one to the next, each removing one layer; the one who removes the final layer keeps the prize)
passage (*see* passageway)	hall, hallway, corridor
passageway (*see* passage)	hall, hallway, corridor
past (*ten ... two*)	after
past master	a person with great talent or experience

English	American
past sell-by date (see sell-by date)	over the hill, no longer useful
pasty (see Cornish pasty)	pastry filled with meat, onions, potatoes and vegetables
pat of butter	small portion
patch (a bad ...)	time
pavement (see footpath)	sidewalk
pavement princess	prostitute who advertises over CB radio
paw paw	papaya
pay in (... ... account)	deposit
pay on the nail (see stump up)	pay up (on the spot)
paymaster	donor funding sources
peak time (aired at ... ...)	prime time
peaky	looking pale and sickly, under the weather
pear shaped (go ... ...)	badly wrong
peas above sticks	too big for one's britches

pea souper

English	American
pea-souper	thick fog
pecker (*keep your ... up*)	chin, spirits
peckish	hungry
pee (*take a ...*)	piss, use the toilet
peed off	pissed off
peer (*peeress*)	nobleman or woman, who hold a title (formerly, all peers were members of the House of Lords, but today one may hold the title but not be in the House of Lords)

English	American
peg(ging) (... *the laundry*)	hang clothing on a (clothes) line using clothes pins
peg out	die
pelican crossing	crosswalk with stoplight and pedestrian button
pen (*v.*) (... *a note*)	write
pen friend	pen pal
pending tray	container where pending matters are kept
penman	forger
penny dreadful	cheap paperback novel
penny dropped	figured out, saw the light
penny to drop (*waiting for the ... ...*)	understanding, to figure out, see the light
pension off	force someone to retire and receive his or her pension
penultimate	next to last
people carrier	mini-van
Personal assistant (P.A.)	aide
Perspex	Plexiglas

English	American
petrol	gasoline
petrol bomb	home made incendiary device consisting of a bottle filled with gasoline
petrol station	gas station, service station
pettifogger (*n.*) (*see* pettifoggery)	one who engages in sharp practice, usually in reference to a lawyer
pettifoggery (*engaged in* ...) (*see* pettifogger)	sharp practice, quibbling, petty, dishonest
phone box (*see* call box, phone kiosk)	phone booth
phone kiosk (*see* call box, phone box)	phone booth
photo call	public book signing by an author with photographs taken
physio (*abbr.* physiotherapist) .	athletic trainer
physiotherapist (*see* physio)	athletic trainer
pibroch	form of bagpipe music
pic (*pl.* pix)	photograph(s)
pick up on it (*... her ... ...*)	correct, point out an error

English	American
pickings	easy money
pictures (*went to the ...*)	movies, cinema
piddle (*see* jimmy riddle, slash, tiddle, widdle)	urinate
pies	traditional English food, pastry crust with savoury or sweet fillings
piffle	nonsense
pigeon post	internal mail (*e.g.* campus mail)
pigeonhole	open mail receptacle
pig sick	absolutely fed up
piggy in the middle	stuck in between two people who are arguing
pig's breakfast (*see* dog's breakfast)	mess
pillarbox (*see* letterbox)	upright cylindrical mailbox
pillock	jerk
pin (*didn't give one ...*)	anything at all, nothing
pinafore (*see* pinny)	apron
pinch	steal

English	American
pinch of salt	grain of salt
pindown	confine children in care with restrictions
pink (*in the ...*)	in good health
pinny (*see* pinafore)	apron
pin-splitter	a fine golf shot
pip (*give someone the ...*)	annoy
pipped at the post (*racing metaphor*)	beaten at the last minute, nosed out
piss about	mess around
piss off	get lost
pissed	intoxicated
piss-up (*n.*)	bungled situation, drinking session
pitch (*n.*) (*rugby ...*)	athletic field
pitch into	attack
plaster	band-aid, adhesive bandage
play the man instead of the ball	seek advantage by tactical ruse

English	American
play up (v.)	aggravate, not work properly
playsuit	child's jumpsuit
PLC	Public Limited Company
plimsolls	deck shoes, sneakers
plonk	cheap wine
plonker	irresponsible person
ploughman's lunch	lump of bread, cheese and pickle
PLU	people like us
pluck (*had the ...*)	courage
pluck up	summon up courage
plug hole	drain
plump (v.) (*... for*)	choose, pick out, vote
plus-fours	pants gathered in at the knee
PM	Prime Minister
po faced	facial expression of misery
point (*see power point*)	electrical outlet, socket

English	American
point-to-point	cross country horse racing from one point to another
polenta	savory rice pudding-like dish
police van	police vehicle used to transport persons (to the police station)
poly (*abbr.* polytechnic)	college offering courses at and below degree level
Polyfilla	Spackle, filler paste to patch walls
polytechnic (see poly)	college offering courses at and below degree level
pom (*abbr.* pommy)	Australian, New Zealand term for person from Britain
pommy (see pom)	Australian, New Zealand term for person from Britain
Pomponian	person from Portsmouth
ponce (*n.*)	effeminate manner
poncey (*adj.*)	in an effeminate manner
pong (see niffy, whiffy)	bad smell
pony	twenty-five pounds sterling
pony up	pay up

English	American
poodle	obedient, responds absolutely
poodle about	wander about aimlessly
poodle faker	ladies' man
poof (*abbr.* poofter)	male homosexual
poofter (*see* poof)	male homosexual
poorly (*He's right ...*)	ill, very ill
pooter	blood-sucking insect
pop (*... it in*)	put in
pop around (*see* pop in)	pay a quick visit, drop in, go across
pop in (*see* pop around)	pay a quick visit, drop in. go across

pop your clogs

pop your clogs	die
poppet	a cute child
Poppy Day	Memorial Day
pork pie	cooked pork with pastry crust
pork scratchings	pork flavored potato chips
porky pies	lies

English	American
porridge	oatmeal
portcullis	grating above castle gate that can be lowered to block the entrance
porter	caretaker
porter	heavy, Guinness-like beer
porterage	moving items from one place to another
portfolio (*see* without portfolio)	area of responsibility of a minister of state
posh	upper class
position (*the ... is*)	pronoun other than *the* used before *position* in American English
post (*n.*)	mail
post (*v.*)	to mail
post code	zip code
post room	mail room
postal order	money order
postbag	mailman's bag
postman	mailman

English	American
posts	goalposts
potholing	exploring underground caves
potted	convicted in court
potted (*adj.*) (*... history*)	short, brief
potted (*v.*) (*snooker*)	hit a ball into a pocket
potter about	puttering around
potty (*go completely ...*)	crazy
poulterer	one who sells poultry
pound	monetary unit of Great Britain
power cut	power loss
power point (*see point*)	electrical outlet, socket
practising certificate	license to practice
pram	baby buggy
prang (*n.*)	automobile accident
pranged	wrecked
prat	fool, stupid person
prawn	shrimp

English	American
preen (v.)	show off
preg (see preggers, preggy, banged up, in the club, up the duff)	pregnant
preggers (see preg, preggy, banged up, in the club, up the duff	pregnant
preggy (see preg, preggers, banged up, in the club, up the duff)	pregnant
presenter	anchorman
press into service	force to be involved
press on (v.)	keep going, go ahead
press ups	push-ups
pressurized (... to act)	pressured
prig (n.)	smugly self-righteous, narrow-minded person
priggish (adj.)	acting like a prig
primary school	elementary school
prise (v.) (... open)	force open
prize	award or honor for academic or athletic achievement in school

English	American
prize giving	award ceremony, usually at school
prod	Protestant
profiterole	creampuff
programme	program
promenade	boardwalk
promenade concert	concert where some of the audience stands rather than sits
Proms	BBC's summer music festival at Royal Albert Hall in London
pronk	weak person
prosty	prostitute
pseud	pretentious person, phony
pub (see public house)	bar, tavern
pub lunch	light lunch served in a pub
public footpath	public access to walk across private land
public house (see pub)	bar, tavern
public school	private school

English	American
public schoolboy	preppie
publican	manager of a bar
pucker	the real thing
pudding	dessert
puffa jacket	heavily quilted jacket
puffin crossing	pedestrian crosswalk with sensor to regulate traffic
pukka (... *gent*)	aristocratic, upper class
pull a stroke	pull a fast one, cheat someone
pull down (*see* knock down)	tear down, demolish
pull you up	call a matter to one's attention, criticize

punch-up

punch-up	fight
punt (*n.*)	small flat bottomed boat
punt (*v.*)	place a bet
punter	one who places a bet, a customer
punting	to ride in a punt
purse	change purse
purser	staff in charge of passengers on board a plane or ship
push (*the ...*)	losing one's job
push off (*he will ... ...*)	take off, head off, leave

English	American
push the boat out	being more extravagant than usual
pushchair	baby stroller
pushed	lost job, fired
push-like (... *resources*)	scanty, meager
put across	express successfully
put a foot wrong	done something wrong
put a sock in it	keep your mouth shut
put down (*v.*) (*animal*)	put to sleep
put down (*v.*) (*goods*)	charge
put forward	make a statement, proposal
put right	fix, correct
put the boot in	do something aggressively and enthusiastically (*e.g.* overpower opponent)
put the mockers on	ruin chances for success
put the wind up	scare, frighten
put through (*telephone*)	transfer a telephone call to another person

English	American
put up (... ... *for*)	nominate
put up prices	raise, increase
put upon	taken advantage of

Q

QC (*see* silk)	Queen's Counsel
Q.E.D.	which was the thing to be proved, I rest my case
quaff	drink heartily
quango	unelected government regulatory agency
quantity surveyor	one who estimates the cost of a construction job
quarter of an hour	fifteen minutes
quay	pier, wharf
queen(y)	effeminate gay man
queue (*n.*)	line

queue

English	American
queue (*v.*)	stand in line
quid	one pound sterling
quid's in	money is in hand (usually a profitable situation)
quiet (*on the ...*)	on the q.t.
quit	leave, vacate
quite (*yes, ...*)	yes, expression of affirmation or agreement
quite right	agreed
quod	jail
quoit	something tossed in a game of accuracy

English	American
R	
rabbit on (*see* rabbiting)	talk too much
rabbit pie	cooked rabbit with pastry crust
rabbiting	hunting rabbits
rabbiting (*see* rabbit on)	talking too much
rack and ruin (*go to* ... ...)	be destroyed
racy (*... book*)	daring (with sexual connotation)
radiotherapy	radiation (treatment)
rail (*clothing*) (*off the ...*)	rack
railway	railroad
railway station	train station, railroad station
ram (*a ...*)	rear end collision

rambler

rambler	one who walks through the countryside
ram-raiding	crashing a car into a store and stealing merchandise
randy	horny
rarebit (*see* Welsh rarebit)	toast covered with mixture of melted cheese and milk
rasher	slice of bacon
rat run	rat race
rat-arsed	drunk
ratbag	worthless person

English	American
rate payer(s)	taxpayer(s)
ratty	irritable
rave (*n.*)	a crush on someone
Rawlplug	anchor device to affix object to floor or wall
readies (*come up with the ...*)	money
read(ing) (*... history at university*)	major in, study
real ale	beer which is still fermenting (should be kept cold but not chilled)
receipt (*personal ... of*)	recipe
reception	front desk
recorded delivery	certified mail
red pepper (*see green pepper*)	bell pepper
red tape	cloth binding around an official document (especially a legal document)

English	American
redbrick (*adj.*)	any of the English universities founded in the late 1800s or early 1900s (*i.e.* not Oxford or Cambridge)
redirect (*mail*)	forward
redundant	unemployed
refectory	cafeteria, dining room (usually at a college or university)
register (*take the ...*)	roll, attendance
registered post	registered mail
relations	relatives
remand centre	place where accused person is detained pending trial, holding cell
Remembrance Day	Veteran's Day (November 11)
removal man	mover
require (*will ...*)	need
residence (*legal*)	custody of minor children
resile (we must not ...)	recoil or retreat
resit (*... the exam*)	retake

English	American
restricted speed area	speed zone
return ticket	ticket to destination and back, round trip
returning officer	an election official (in charge of election returns)
reverse charges	call collect
reversing lights	back up lights
revise (... for exams)	review, study
ribby (adj.)	shabby, run-down
rich (comes a bit ...)	a rather far-fetched statement, presumptuous
Richmond Maids of Honor	custard almond cakes
rick	swindler's accomplice (e.g. to drive up the bidding at an auction)
right (Oh ...) (upon hearing the unexpected)	Oh, my; Oh, really
ring (n.)	telephone call
ring (v.) (please ...) (see ring up)	call on the telephone
ring fence (v.)	set aside (e.g. money) for a specific purpose

English	American
ring off	end a telephone call
ring road	bypass
ring round	telephone survey
ring up (v.) (see ring)	call on the telephone
ripper (real ...)	very good
ripping	terrific, cool
ripping yarn	great story
rise (n.)	raise, increase (usually in salary)
rise (v.)	stand up
rise out of (take a ... ...)	get a rise out of
rise to the bait	rise to the occasion
risible	causing laughter
rising (age)(... seventy-five)	approaching
road	highway
road accident (see road crash)	highway accident
road crash (see road accident)	highway accident

English	American
road metal	broken stones used in building highways
road safety	highway safety
rock cake	small fruitcake with a rough surface
rockery	display of stones with flowers
rockery plants	plants which grow out of rocks
rocket	broad-leafed herb used like lettuce
rocket (*give someone a ...*)	telling off
rocket salad	green leaf salad
roger (*to ...*)	have sexual intercourse
roller	Rolls Royce car
rollicking (*see bollocking*)	tell someone off
roof (*car*)	top
roofing felt (*see felt*)	lining under shingle
room (*come to my ...*)	office
root and branch (*... ... ... changes*)	thoroughly, the whole thing

English	American
ropy	poor quality
ropy (*finances pretty ...*)	not good
rosy	drunk
rotter (*see* blighter)	despicable person
round (*drop this ...*)	off
round (*one way ...*)	around
round brackets (*see* bracket)	parentheses
round the bend	crazy
round the twist (*drive me ... ...*)	crazy, mad
roundabout	intersection, traffic circle
rounded on (*he ... ... her*)	criticize severely
rounder (*see* rounders)	home run in rounders
rounders	game similar to baseball
rout	wild party
row (*n.*) (*see* ruck)	argument
row (*v.*)	argue noisily
rowan	mountain ash (tree)

English	American
royal warrant	special designation given by any member of the Royal Family to supplier of products who is allowed to display an appropriate coat of arms
rubber	eraser
rubbish	trash
rubbish (*see* dross)	spoken or written words that are of little value, nonsense
rubbish (*v.*) (*to ...*)	destroy, trash
rubbish bin	trash can, waste basket
rubbish tip (*see* midden, tip)	trash dump
rubbishing	dismiss as without merit
ruck (*n.*) (*see* row)	argument
ruck (*rugby metaphor*)	rough crowd of people
rucksack	backpack
ructious (*n.*)	disturbance
rude (*... health*)	good, wholesome, sturdy

rugger

rugger (*play* ...)	rugby (game with features of both American football and soccer, originated at Rugby School, Rugby, England)
rumbled	to see through (a deception), found out
rumpers (*in* ...)	diapers
rumpy-pumpy (*see other*)	hanky-panky
running (*two weeks* ...)	in a row
run-up (*n.*)	the run taken by a bowler in cricket before he bowls the ball

English	American
run-up (*n.*) (*cricket metaphor*) (... ... to the election)	period of time immediately preceding an event (when preparation takes place)

S

sack (*get the ...*) (*see* get the bullet, get the push, get your cards)	fired
sacked	fired, dismissed
St. George's Day	April 23, to honor St. George, the patron saint of England
St. Martin's summer	Indian summer
Sally Army	Salvation Army
saloon car	four-door car
salt beef	corned beef
saltcellar	saltshaker
sandpit	sandbox
sarnies	sandwiches
sauce (*chocolate ...*)	syrup
saucepan	cooking pan with a handle

English	American
Saville Row suit	high quality, tailor-made man's suit
savouries	tasty snacks
savoy	variety of cabbage
saw a bit off	sexual intercourse
scarper	run away or leave quickly

scarper

scatty	spacey, empty headed
scoff	food
scoff (v.)	eat hungrily

English	American
scone	half way between cake and biscuit – harder than a cake but softer than a biscuit and served with butter and jam or clotted cream
Scotch eggs	hard boiled egg surrounded by a meatball with breadcrumbs (common in pubs)
Scouser	person from Liverpool
scrag-end	undesirable part
scratch (*up to ...*)	up to standard
scratch card	lottery ticket
scratchy	bitchy
scribbling pad	scratch pad
script (*student*)	examination paper
scrotty	crummy
scrubber	woman of loose morals
scrubs up well	cleans up well
scrum (*rugby metaphor*)	mass of people
scupper	prostitute

English	American
scuppered	prevented from doing something
sea	ocean
second bite of the cherry	another opportunity, second bite of the apple
secondment	leave of absence
second year (*undergraduate*)	sophomore
see a bit off	sexual intercourse
seen off	sports team routed by opponent
sell up	sell out
sell-by date (see past sell-by date)	expiration date
Sellotape	Scotch tape
semi-detached house	house joined to another house, duplex
semolina	cream of wheat
send down	send to prison
send-up (*n.*)	imitation (satirical), parody
send up (*v.*)	making fun of a person, satirize

English	American
sent down (*Oxbridge*)	dismissed from school
sent off	kicked out, disqualified from competition
sent to Coventry	ignored by associates or colleagues

Sent to Coventry

English	American
service flats	apartment hotel (self-catering)
serviette	table napkin
set down (*passenger ... ...*)	dropped off
setpiece (*rugby metaphor*)	uninterrupted
settee	couch, love seat
sex on a stick	sexy person
sex up	intentional exaggeration of truth

English	American
shadow government	the opposition to the government, i.e. the party in control of Parliament
shadow minister	opposition minister who "shadows" government minister
shag (v.)	have sexual intercourse
shagged	worn out
shaken sheet	rippled
shambolic (adj.) (... plan)	disastrous
shandy	beer and lemonade drink
shank's pony	on foot
shan't	shall not
shares	stocks
share shop	brokerage firm
sharp end	what it's really like, place where it's all happening
shattered	tired, exhausted
shaving tackle	razor, soap and brush
sheet anchor (sailing metaphor)	steady, reliable, solid (person or thing), a mainstay

English	American
shemozzle	uproar, commotion
shepherd's pie	cooked meat covered with mashed potatoes
shilling (*not the full ...*)	not the whole thing or full amount, not all there
shilly-shally	delay, waste time
shin up	climb up
shinning	climbing or advancing upward
ship shape in Bristol fashion	everything precisely in order, in ship shape
shire	county
shirt-lifter	homosexual
shirty	annoyed, angry, ready to fight
shit-bag	despicable person, shit head
shoelace	shoestring
shoe mender	shoe repair
shooter	gun
shop	store

English	American
shop assistant (*see* floor walker)	sales clerk
shopfront	storefront
short and curleys (*got them by the ... ...*)	testicles, balls (or hair thereon)
short back and sides	close haircut
short straw (*bit of a ... ...*)	bad luck
shout (*give me a ...*)	get in touch, give me a holler
show jumper	show jumping horse
shower	worthless and unpleasant person or group of people
Shrove Tuesday	day before Ash Wednesday
shut (*the store is ...*)	closed
shut your gob	shut your mouth
sick as a parrot	very sick
side (*sport*)	team
sideboards	sideburns
sidey	conceited

English	American
silencer (*car*)	muffler
silk (*see* QC)	Queen's Counsel
sill (*motor car*)	rocker panel (car)
silly billy	foolish person
sin bin (*sport*)	penalty
single handed	on your own
single ticket	one way ticket
singlet	sleeveless T-shirt
sitting room	living room
sixes and sevens	state of confusion, disarray
sixth form	further course of study for seventeen and eighteen-year-old students preparing for work, college or university
skeleton in your cupboard	skeleton in your closet
skidpan	specially designed area made slippery for drivers to practice controlling skids
Skinny Liz	thin woman
skint	without money

English	American
skip (... *containing rubbish*)	large steel container, dumpster
skipper	captain of sports team
skipping rope	jump rope
skirting board	baseboard
skittles	game in which player tries to knock down pins (skittles) by rolling a ball at them
skived off (*v.*)	avoided work, took a day off
skiver (*n.*)	one who avoids work
slag	whore, slut
slagging off	nasty criticism
slam-door (*n.*)	older train with manually operated doors
slanging (... *match*)	exchanging insults
slap (*put on some ...*)	makeup
slapper	loose woman
slash (*v.*) (*take a ...*) (*male*) (*see* jimmy riddle, piddle, tiddle, widdle)	urinate
slattern (*a real ...*)	slovenly

English	American
sledging	sledding
sledging	trash talk (during sports competition)
sleeper	railroad tie
sleeper	sleeping pill
sleeping car	Pullman
sleeping policeman	speed bump
sleeping rough	sleeping in the street
sliced loaf	loaf previously sliced
slide (see hair slide)	barrette
slip road	on or off ramp
slipper (v.)	paddling, trashing
Sloan ranger	attractive, superficial, well-to-do young woman
slog (n.)	hard work
slog (v.) (... the ball)	hit hard
slope off	sneak off
slusher (see cobbler, monopoly man)	counterfeiter

English	American
slut (*dirty ...*)	slovenly woman (not sexual)
sluttish (*... behavior*)	slovenly female (not sexual)
small beer	small potatoes, insignificant
small hours	early hours
smalls (*washing ...*)	underwear
smarm (*v.*) (*... his way*)	ingratiate oneself, charm
smarmy (*adj.*)	obsequious, fawning
smart	well dressed
smash and grab	robbery
smasher	an attractive man or woman
smashing (*that's ...*)	very good
snack van	van or bus converted for selling food and beverages at roadside rest stops
snaffle (*to ...*)	steal
snaffle up	gobble, grab
snakes and ladders	ups and downs

English	American
snap	photograph
snigger	snicker
snip (*at a ...*)	reduced price
snog	big, juicy kiss
snuff it	die
snug	area or room away from the bar in a pub
sobriquet	nickname
sod	obnoxious person, idiot
sod it (*Oh, ...!*)	to heck (hell) with it, screw it
sod-all	nothing
Sod's Law	Murphy's Law (if something can go wrong it will go wrong)
soft (*... on someone*)	like another person
soft in the head	stupid
soldier on	keep up an effort
soldiers (*see* Marmite soldiers)	slice of bread cut into fingers
solicitor	attorney, lawyer

English	American
sop (v.)	make a concession, placate, sell out
sorbet (see ice)	sherbet
Sorry	Excuse me (an apology)
Sorry?	Excuse me (I didn't hear you)
sort out	work out, arrange, organize
sorted (that's been ...)	worked out, arranged, organized
soundings (taking ...)	getting the general view on a subject

Soup-strainer

soup-strainer	long mustache
sozzle (v.)	drink alcoholic beverage
sozzled	drunk
spaggers	spaghetti
spaghetti junction	cloverleaf
spanner	wrench (open or adjustable)
spanner in the works	disruption, an obstacle, throw a wrench into a situation

English	American
spark (see lecky man)	alarm expert, technician
spark out	out cold, unconscious
sparkler	gemstone
sparkling plug	sparkplug
sparks	electrician
speciality	specialty
specs (abbr. spectacles)	glasses
spend a penny (v.) (female)	go to the toilet
spew (see hurling)	vomit, throw up
spiffing	marvelous, outstanding
spillage (n.) (oil ...)	spill
spin a coin	flip or toss a coin
spin out	prolong
spiv	slick dressed, shady character
splash me boots (male)	go to the toilet
splash out	blow money, make substantial investment or advance

English	American
split-ticketing	ticket-splitting
sport	athletics, sports
sporting chance	some possibility of success
sporty	enjoys athletics (sports)
spot (... of)	small quantity
spot of bother	little bit of trouble
spot-on (see bang-on)	exactly right
spotted dick	pudding made of suet and raisins
spout (v.)	talk nonsense
spouting (n.)	eaves trough
spring onions	scallions
sprog	child
sprog	junior colleague (condescending)
square brackets (see bracket)	brackets

square eyes

square eyes	watching too much television
squash (*drink*)	juice
squeak (*narrow ...*)	narrow escape
squire	country gentleman; chief landed proprietor in a district
squirearchy	landowners collectively
staff (*academic*)	faculty
stair rods (*coming down ... ...*)	raining cats and dogs
stalls (*theatre*)	orchestra seats
stand (*airport*)	gate

English	American
stand (*... for public office*)	run for office
stand down	step down, resign
standard	acceptable quality
standard lamp	floor lamp
staring me out	staring me down
starkers	stark naked
start again	start over
starter	appetizer
state of play	state of affairs, status of things
state school	public school
stationer	store which sells writing supplies as well as books, newspapers, etc.
stay stum (*see* stum)	keep quiet
steak and kidney pie (*see* kidney pudding)	chunks of beef and lamb kidney in gravy with pastry crust
steeplejack	a person who builds or repairs church steeples and chimneys
sterling	British monetary system

English	American
stick	cane
stick (*gave me some ...*)	grief, a hard time, told off, criticized
sticking plaster	adhesive tape
sticky wicket (*cricket metaphor*)	difficult situation
stile	steps allowing people to climb a fence or wall
still as a mill pond	very still
stingo	a very strong Yorkshire ale
stitch him up	told on person, snitch
stitch-up (*n.*)	behind the scenes deal
stock cube	bouillon cube
stock-still	motionless
stone (*fruit*)	pit
stone (*weight*)	fourteen pounds
Stone the crows!	Holy cow!
stonking (*a ... good time*)	excellent, very good
stony-broke	stone broke

English	American
stop press	breaking news item
stopcock	tap to water main
storming (*adj.*)	exceptionally well played
straight on	straight ahead
straightaway	right away, right now
strap hanging	standing in bus or train holding on to straps provided
straw boater	straw hat
streaky bacon	bacon with streaks of fat
street (*by a ...*)	long distance
streets ahead (*... ... of the others*)	far ahead of, superior to
stress puppy	person who habitually complains
strides	pants, trousers
strip (*n.*)	athletic uniform
stripling	young person
stroke	diagonal line
strongroom	vault

English	American
stroppy	difficult, argumentative
struck off	name removed from list and job lost (usually in medical profession)
stuck in the sidings	left behind
stud (*athletic shoe*)	cleat, spike
studio	efficiency
stuff (*couldn't care a ...*)	couldn't care less
stuff all (*I know ... ...*)	don't know anything
stuffed to the gunnels	packed
stum (*see stay stum*)	quiet
stump up (*see pay on the nail*)	pay up
stumped (*cricket metaphor*)	stuck, halted
sub (*v.*)	pay someone money on account
subjects	citizens
submission (*court*)	formal request, statement
subscription (*see voluntary subscription*)	membership

English	American
subway	underground walkway
Suffolk punch	a draft horse, bred for heavy farm work, etc.
suit me down to the ground	would be perfect, ideal
suited and booted	dressed up, dressed to kill
sultana	raisin
sump	oil pan in car
sums (*read, write and do ...*)	arithmetic
super	police superintendent
superstore	supermarket
sure as eggs is eggs	without any doubt
surgery hours (*doctor, dentist*)	office hours
surgical spirit	rubbing alcohol
surname	last name
suspender belt (*see* suspenders)	garter belt
suspenders (*see* suspender belt)	garter belt

English	American
suss (v.)	think or work out
sussed (adj.)	informed
swag	stolen property
swamping	too much concentrated ethnic diversity in deprived areas of the inner city
swan about (v.) (see swanning)	wander about idly
swank (he's a …)	boastful person, show-off
swanning (see swan about)	wandering about idly
swede	turnip
sweet shop	candy store
sweets	candy
swimming bath	swimming pool
swimmingly	moving along or going well
swing (take a …)	chance
swing the lead	attempt to gain an advantage by deceit
swingeing	wide sweeping, far reaching

English	American
swings and roundabouts	six of one, half dozen of the other, makes no difference
swish	in style, sharp
Swiss roll	jelly roll
switch off (... ... *the light*)	turn off
switch solo	debit card
switched off	relaxing
switched on	neat, sharp, together person
swiz (*abbr.* swizzle)	swindle
swot (*n.*)	person who studies hard
swot (*v.*)	study hard

T

ta	thank you
ta ta for now (*see* tatty bye)	goodbye for now, see you later
table (*v.*)	to bring something forward for discussion

English	American
tablets (*on ...*)	medication
tack	riding harness, saddles, etc.
tack room	room where riding harnesses, saddles, etc. are kept
tackle	male genitalia
taffy	Welsh person
tail to teeth	from beginning to end, A to Z
tailback	traffic jam
tailboard	back panel of a truck
take a view	take a position
take in	pay attention to
take instructions	consult
take it or lump it	take it or leave it
take no notice	disregard, pay no attention to
take notice	pay attention to
take on board (*need to ... ...*)	consider seriously

English	American
take the piss (*see* mickey)	tease or kid another person
take your position	take your seat
takeaway (*n.*)	a restaurant that sells food to go
takeaway (*n.*)	carry out food, a take home meal
takes the bisquit	takes the cake
taking (*... decisions*)	making
takings	proceeds from sale, receipts
tall story	tall tale
Tally ho!	Let's go!
tallyman	debt collector
tap	faucet
tap room	a room in a pub where the barrels were once kept
tariff	list of prices
tarmac (*airport*)	ramp
tart up	dress in a flashy or tasteless fashion

English	American
tattie	potato
tattoo	military display, pageant
tatty	threadbare, worn out, in tatters
tatty bye (*see ta ta for now*)	goodbye, bye bye
tea and sympathy	token words of comfort
tea cake	a type of cake with sultanas, toasted and spread with butter
tea cosy	cloth covering for a teapot to keep the tea warm
tea lady	person in an office who serves tea from a trolley
tea towel	dish towel
tear off a strip (*... someone ... ...*)	tell someone off, reprimand
teat	nipple
tee up (*golfing metaphor*)	schedule an event
telephone box	telephone booth, phone booth
telly	television, TV
ten a penny	common

English	American
tenner	ten pound note
term (*school*)	semester, quarter
terrestrial (*... TV*)	non-cable TV channels
Territorial Army	similar to National Guard
tetchy (*... relations*)	strained, tense, irritable
thatch (*losing my ...*)	hair
thick (*a bit ...*)	unfair, unreasonable
thick as two short posts	stupid, thick, dumb as dirt
thick on the ground	a lot
thin end of the wedge	that which leads to something more significant (usually a problem), opening Pandora's Box, opening a can of worms
third degree (*n.*) (*university*)	fourth highest rank in British university degree classification system (roughly comparable to C- grade in U.S.)
third year (*undergraduate*)	junior
thorn in my flesh	thorn in my side
throaty	hoarse

English	American
throw a wobbly	be upset, throw a tantrum
throw in's distance (*football metaphor*)	a short distance
thumping good	very good
thunder and lightning	clotted cream and black treacle (molasses) spread on freshly baked bread
tick (*on ...*)	credit
tick (*one ...*)	a moment
tick box (*see* tick mark)	box on a document where check mark placed
tick it on	put on credit
tick mark (*see* tick box)	check mark
tickover	idling like a car, just getting by
tiddle (*see* jimmy riddle, piddle, slash, widdle)	urinate
tiddler	something very small (usually used in reference to a fish)
tiddly	slightly intoxicated
tiddly	very small

English	American
tied house	pub owned by a brewery and required to sell its products
tights	panty hose
till	cash register
tiller (*hand on the ...*)	steering the ship, calling the shots, in control, involved in directing policy
time-table (*train ...*)	schedule
tin	can
tin loaf	square loaf
tin pot	worthless, unimportant
tinkle	call on telephone
tinned	canned
tinned food	canned food
tip (*see* rubbish tip, midden)	dump, trash dump
tipper truck	dump truck
tipping down (*it's ... ...*)	pouring (rain)
tipple	one's favorite alcoholic drink

English	American
Tipstaff	officer of the Supreme Court (*i.e.* High Court and Court of Appeal) mainly concerned with arresting and escorting to prison people who are guilty of contempt or recovering children wrongly removed from their care-givers
tiswas (*see* tizz-wozz)	flap or panic
tit-bit	tidbit
title deed	deed
tits up	belly up, bust, failure
tiz (*tizzy*)	confused or agitated state
tiz-wozz (*see* tiswas)	flap or panic
to a penny	precisely, completely
to twig	sudden understanding
toadies	ingratiating persons
toad-in-the-hole	sausages baked in batter
toady (*see* arse-licker, bum-licker)	ingratiating person, ass-kisser, brown-nose
toadying	be ingratiating, kissing ass
tobacconist	tobacco store

English	American
tocsin	alarm signal or bell
toe rag	contemptible person
toff (*see* nob)	upper class person
toffed up	well dressed
toffee	taffy
toffee-nose	snob
toffee-nosed	snobbish
toggle	piece of wood which fits through a loophole on an overcoat, button
toilet	bathroom, restroom
toilet bag	bag which contains toiletries, personal items
tomfoolery (*n.*)	foolish behavior
too big for your boots	too big for your britches
toodle pip (*see* cheerio, cheers)	goodbye, so long
took a job upstairs	died
tootle along (*... ... in a motor car*)	driving happily

English	American
top (*... of the street*)	beginning
top (*v.*)	kill
top (*... himself*)	commit suicide
top copy (*document*)	original
top of the morning	good morning
top of the stack (*see top of the tree*)	top of the heap
top of the tree (*see top of the stack*)	top of the heap

top shelf magazine

top shelf magazine	pornographic magazine
top table (n.) (*see* high table)	head table
top to toe	top to bottom
top up	fill up

English	American
top-dress	spread fertilizer on the land
torch	flashlight
tosh	nonsense or rubbish
toss (*don't give a ...*)	don't give a damn
tosser (*see wanker*)	jerk
tot up	add numbers
totter	dealer in scrap metal
totty (*n.*)	loose girl or woman
touch wood (*see grip wood*)	knock on wood, hopeful
tough as old boots	tough as nails
tout (*n.*)	scalper
tout (*v.*)	sell ticket at inflated price, scalping
town centre (*see city centre*)	downtown
trade union	labor union
tradesman	one engaged in trade (*e.g.* a shopkeeper)
tradesman's entrance	delivery entrance

English	American
traffic calming device	concrete barrier to slow traffic, speed bump
traffic calming measures	installation of speed bump
traffic lights	stop lights
traffic warden (see warden)	person who issues parking tickets
trailer	vehicle pulled by a car and used for transporting large or small items
trainers	sneakers, athletic shoes
tram	streetcar
tray	in or out receptacle on office desk
treacle (see black treacle)	molasses
tred the boards	act on stage
trifle	sponge cake with jam, fruit, cream and custard (sherry sometimes added)
tripper (see day tripper)	tourist
trog	obnoxious person, jerk
trolley (off her ...)	off her rocker
trolley (shopping ...)	cart

English	American
trousers	pants, slacks
trout (*old ...*)	crotchety, ill-tempered older person
trumps (*turned up ...*)	decked out
truncheon	police officer's night stick
trunk call	long distance call
trunk road	main road
tube (*see* underground)	subway
tuck (*see* tucker)	food
tuck shop	store that sells food
tucker (*see* tuck)	food
tumble to	work out, figure out
tup (*v.*)	man having intercourse with a woman
tuppence (*care a ...*)	not much
turf	horse racing
turf accountant	bookmaker
turf out	throw out
turn-ups (*... ... on trousers*)	cuffs

English	American
twaddle (*load of ...*) (see twiddle twaddle)	rubbish, bunch of baloney
twee	too cute or sweet
twenty to the dozen (*talking ... ...*)	talking fast
twiddle twaddle (see twaddle)	rubbish, bunch of baloney
twig	realize, understand
twit	pompous person
two an' eight	confused, in a state
twock	legal slang term for unlawful taking of a car (taking without owner's consent)
tyre pressure (car)	air pressure (tire)

U

English	American
U (*see* non-U)	behavior acceptable to upper class
U.K.	United Kingdom – composed of England, Wales, Scotland and Northern Ireland

English	American
unawares (*he caught me ...*)	unaware, by surprise
Uncle Tom Cobbley and all	everybody

Uncle Tom Cobbley and all

English	American
under the cosh	under pressure
undercarriage	landing gear of airplane
underdrawers	underwear, undies
underground (*see* tube)	subway
understairs cupboard	closet
undertakings	commitments
unit trust	mutual fund

English	American
up(ping) (... *the cost*)	increase, raise
up a gum tree	stuck, up a creek
up market	expensive
up one's nose	aggravating, irritating
up sticks	getting up and around
up the duff (*see* banged up, in the club, preg, preggers, preggy)	pregnant
up the Kyber	up a creek, out of luck
up the spout	gone wrong, pregnant
up to scratch	up to par, up to the job
up to the eyes	up to the earlobes
uppers (*on his ...*)	having no money
upper second degree (2.1)	second highest rank in British university degree classification system (roughly comparable to B/B+ grade in U.S.)
upstanding (*see* be upstanding)	rise, stand up
usher	court official

English	American
value for money (*good ... ...*)	bargain
valve (*radio*)	tube
van	delivery truck
VAT (*abbr.* value added tax)	sales tax
verger	vicar's assistant (C of E), church caretaker
vest	undershirt
vet (*v.*)	investigate a person

veterinary surgeon

English	American
veterinary surgeon	veterinarian
vexed question	much debated topic

English	American
vicar	minister
vicarage	residence of minister
vice chancellor (*university*)	president
Victorian	pertaining to the reign of Queen Victoria (1837-1901)
victual	food, provisions
victualler (*licensed ...*)	licensed to sell alcoholic beverages
video	VCR
voluntary subscription (*see* subscription)	membership dues

W

wacked	tired, worn out
wadge	a quantity, amount of something, batch, wad of money
wag	witty person
waistcoat	vest
walkabout	a public figure walking among people

English	American
walkout	sexual affair
walkover	easy opponent
wallet	file folder
wallop (*pint of ...*)	beer
wally (*see* charlie, wuss)	stupid person, idiot
wank	male masturbation
wanker (*see* tosser)	jerk
wanky	contemptible
warden (*see* traffic warden)	person who issues parking tickets; the heads of some university colleges have the title of warden
warder	prison guard
wardrobe	closet
wash up (*v.*)	do the dishes
washing-up (*n.*)	the dishes
water closet (WC)	room with a toilet, bathroom
water feature	man-made pond, fountain or waterfall

English	American
waterworks	urinary system
way out	exit
wayside	roadside
wazzock	stupid person, fool
wealth coach	financial adviser
wear (*wouldn't ... it*)	tolerate
weathercock	weathervane
wedge open (*... ... the door*)	prop open
wee	pee, piss
weekend (*at the ...*)	on the weekend
well turned out	neatly and well dressed
Wellies (*abbr.* Wellingtons) (*see* gumboots)	waterproof rubber boots (below knee)
Wellingtons (*see* Wellies)	waterproof rubber boots (below knee)
Welsh dresser	hutch, sideboard
Welsh rarebit (*see* rarebit)	toast covered with mixture of melted cheese and milk
went to the wall	financial (or other) collapse

English	American
wet (*adj.*)	effete, ineffectual
wets (*political*)	moderate members of the Conservative Party
whack	fair share
whacked	worn out
whacking (*... great pay rise*)	very, extremely
whacking good	very good
What a carry on!	commotion, too much happening at once
What a palaver!	commotion, too much happening at once
What a to-do!	commotion, too much happening at once
wheedle	coax
wheely bin (*see* dustbin)	garbage can on wheels
wheeze (*tax ...*)	clever idea or scheme
whiffy (*see* niffy, pong)	bad smelling
whilst	while
whinge	complain, whine

English	American
white-arsed	despicable person
white goods	large household appliances
Whitsun	week following Whit Sunday, the seventh Sunday after Easter
whole of (*the ... ...*)	all of
widdle (*see jimmy riddle, piddle, slash, tiddle*)	urinate
wide boy (*see fly boy*)	operates on margin of the law dealing and selling, streetwise shady character
wide of the mark	off center
wigging (*give a ...*) (*see tore off a strip*)	tell someone off
willy	penis
wimpy bar	cafe, hamburger shop
Win-a-Lot (packet of ... ...)	dog food
wind up	to annoy
windcheater	windbreaker
windscreen (*car*)	windshield

English	American
windscreen wiper	windshield wiper
wine bar	place which serves wine, mixed drinks, and snacks
wine merchant	one who buys and sells wines
wing (*motor car*) (*see* arches)	fender (car)
wing mirror	rear view mirror
winker (*see* indicator)	turn signal on a car
winkle	penis
winkle out	discover information with effort, dig out

winkle pickers

winkle pickers	1950s style pointed toe shoes
with a view	with an intention, purpose in mind
without portfolio (*see* portfolio)	no particular defined duties of a minister of state
witness box	witness stand
wobbly (*cricket metaphor*) (*throw a ...*)	to be upset, throw a tantrum

English	American
wobbly (*something has gone ...*)	wrong
wog	person of color (derogatory)
woggle	ring, usually leather, through which the ends of a neckerchief (*e.g.* Boy Scout) are passed
wonky	shaky or unsteady, not working properly
wood (*into the ...*)	woods
wood for the trees	forest for the trees
wooden spoon	prize for being last
woodworm	termite
woofits	not feeling well
woofter	male homosexual
woolly (*adj.*)	unclear, confused
woolly (*n.*)	wool sweater
woolly liberals	bleeding heart liberals
Woolsack	Lord Chancellor's seat in the House of Lords
Woolworths	dime store, five and ten

English	American
work top	counter top
would have done	would have
would have thought (*I ... ...*)	I think, it seems to me
WREN	member of Women's Royal Naval Service
wrong foot (*v.*) (*... ... a person*)	cause a person to make a mistake
wrong side of the blanket (*born on the ... ...*)	illegitimate
wuss (*see* charlie, wally)	stupid person, idiot

Y

Yank	person from the United States, American
Yard	Scotland Yard
yard	open concrete paved area
Yardie (*...-style*)	Scotland Yard
years on	years later

English	American
yob (*abbr.* yobbo) (*see* oik)	aggressive, bad-mannered young person
yobbo (*see* yob, oik)	aggressive, bad-mannered young person
yonks (*for ...*)	years and years, a long time
Yorkie bar	chocolate bar
Yorkshire pudding	light baked batter pudding
Your Lordship	Your Honor (for addressing a judge)
Your Worship	used by the English to address a lay magistrate or mayor (Americans address a magistrate as Your Honor and a mayor as Mr., Mrs. or Ms. Mayor)
Yours aye,	Yours always,
YP (*abbr.* your problem) (*that's ... ...*)	your problem

Z

zebra crossing	pedestrian right-of-way crossing with black and white stripes on the road and a round blinking light

zebra crossing

zed	letter Z
zip	zipper
zip fastener	zipper

Printed in the United States
32754LVS00002B/64-117